25

Rabbi Daniel Yaakov Travis

Praying
with
Joy

Edited by: N. Elbinger
N. Jakubowicz

FELDHEIM PUBLISHERS
JERUSALEM · NEW YORK

Fourth revised edition October 2012

2012 © Copyright
Rabbi Daniel Yaakov Travis

All rights reserved

ISBN 1-59826-26690000

All questions and comments
to the author are welcomed at:
dytravis@actcom.com
or 14/22 Agasi Street, Har Nof, Jerusalem Israel

Make your *simchah* or shul event an occasion your
guests will never forget. Present them with a copy of
Praying With Joy I or ***Praying With Joy II***,
personalized for your event or fund-raiser, now available
at a special discounted price for bulk orders. If you are
ordering 500 or more, you can have a customized
printing of the book, including up to four pages available
for your own use. For more information and to order,
contact the author at **dytravis@actcom.com**

Distributed by:
Feldheim Publishers
P.O.B 43163 / Jerusalem

208 Airport Executive Park
Nanuet NY. 10954

Printed in Israel

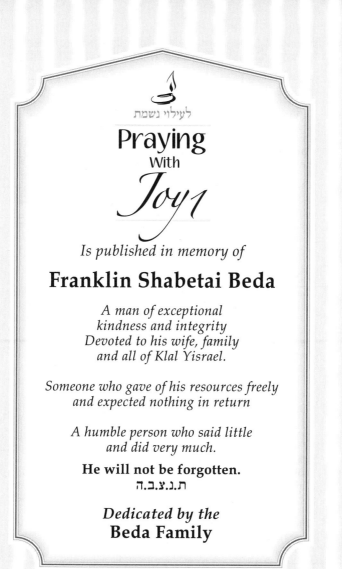

לעילוי נשמת

Praying
With
Joy 1

Is published in memory of

Franklin Shabetai Beda

*A man of exceptional
kindness and integrity
Devoted to his wife, family
and all of Klal Yisrael.*

*Someone who gave of his resources freely
and expected nothing in return*

*A humble person who said little
and did very much.*

He will not be forgotten.
ת.נ.צ.ב.ה.

Dedicated by the
Beda Family

Remembering R' Frank (Shabetai) Beda *z"l*

A Year After His Passing

On the 22nd of *Tammuz* 5771, R' Frank Beda *z"l*, the father of six children, passed away. Frank's *petirah* came towards the start of the Three Weeks, a time when the Jewish people mourn the destruction of the *Bais Hamikdosh.*

When my wife and I heard the news of Frank's untimely death, we were shattered. Just two weeks prior, I had spoken to him on the phone and he had extended me a warm invitation to visit him in his summer home. I just could not believe that Hashem had taken his *neshamah* from this world.

Who will fill the void that Frank Beda left?

I had the great privilege to work with and get to know Frank over the past years. Frank was a humble person, and certainly most of the Jewish people do not know who he was and about his many acts of kindness. I would like to recount a few that I personally witnessed, and I leave the reader to extrapolate and try and formulate a clearer picture of who Frank Beda was.

From His Eulogies

The *Mishnah in Pirkei Avos* says that if a person is liked in this world, he is certainly loved in the next world. In this light, we can understand the *Gemara (Shabbos 153a)* which says, *"From the eulogies of a person, you can tell if he is a ben Olam Haba, if he is headed for the next world."* A number of rabbonim spoke during Frank's *levaya* and *shivah*, and in addition, people wrote about Frank's many attributes during the *shivah*. From their words, it is clear where his soul rests.

One young man related that when he got married, Frank gave him his car as a present. Although this young man was taken aback by this great generosity, he assumed that Frank was anyway buying another car. In truth, he did not purchase another car for eight months, and for this entire time Frank rode the bus.

Frank was dedicated to the *chinuch* of his children and to that of every Jewish child. One of the *rabbeim* of Frank's boys wrote, "As a *rebbi* in the *cheder*, I had quite a number of opportunities to converse with Frank. I was greatly impressed by his devotion to his children and how much it meant to him that they should be filled with and engrossed in Torah, and that their actions should be directed by *yiras Shomayim* and find favor in the eyes of Hashem."

Another person wrote, "While most people gave a gift of money for a newborn, Frank gave *seforim*. I did not understand the value of this until four years after my oldest son was born. I pulled the *seforim "Ko Asu Chachomeinu"* off the shelf and read the stories about the *rabbonim* to my son. What an awesome and thoughtful gift that has immeasurable value. Such was the greatness of his actions - in the way of Torah."

A family member told me that one time, there was a person without any family who was sitting *shivah* in a non-Jewish neighborhood. Frank felt for his situation and decided that if this person did not have any family, **he** was going to be his family. He invited him to sit *shivah* in his home, and made sure people came every day to *daven* and spend time with him.

The Best of Both Worlds

Frank was a rare individual who had one foot firmly planted in the business world and the other foot firmly planted in the *Olam HaTorah*. He lived a life of integrity, and was particularly distressed when he heard that a Torah observant Jew had been involved with business fraud. Frank was especially careful when it came to the *halachos* of *Choshen Mishpat*, and he made it his goal to sanctify Hashem's Name through honest business dealings.

Frank loved Torah, respected *talmidei chachomim,* and had a great desire to learn Torah himself and to strengthen Torah amongst the Jewish people. Whenever Frank spoke about *gedolei Torah* or *talmidei chachomim,* his eyes lit up. We were once walking together with one of his children and he said with a great feeling of pride, "He is going to be a *talmid chochom."*

Frank's kindness was matched by his love of Torah. One *avreich* wrote, "One summer, Shabetai came to learn in the *kollel.* It was so exhilarating to learn with him. I looked forward to arriving in the *kollel.* His questions were probing and dynamic. Our learning became so crystal clear, it was clearly delights from heaven that we were privileged to taste. He brought us joy and happiness. Shabetai was so caring and thoughtful. Whenever we would meet, I felt a genuine love emanating from his *neshamah.* He really cared. He was a holy person, an *ish kadosh."*

Frank believed that the enthusiasm and alacrity that exist in the business world should exist in the *bais medrash.* He especially appreciated the work that we did at Kollel Toras Chaim, training young men to be *talmidei chachomim, poskim,* and leaders of *Klal Yisroel* in all parts of America and the world. Frank was a man of action, and the moment that there was something that could be done for the Jewish people, his interest was piqued.

Emulating Avrohom Avinu

Everyone knows that the tent of Avrohom Avinu had four doors, one on each side. This was more than a gesture. Avrohom wanted to show that, in truth, his house had no walls, and that he wanted to do as much *chessed* as possible. Such was the kindness of Frank Beda.

One young lady wrote, "I used to always feel welcome in his home. I felt so welcome that I would invite my friends to his house. He was a *tzaddik* like Avrohom Avinu, always having guests over. I am sure that Hashem is enjoying his *neshamah.* It is such a pure and beautiful soul. He always loved to learn and go to *shul.* Frank always inspired me to be more religious. I feel I became a better person because he was part of my life. I am happy to have had the opportunity to have known him."

Avrohom Avinu had a *bris milah* when he was one hundred years old. He was certainly exempt from doing *chessed* after such a painful surgery, but his attribute of *chessed* would not let him rest. This urge to do kindness describes the *chessed* of Frank Beda, who was always looking for new opportunities to give of his money and his self.

Good Feelings

Chazal tell us that it is better to give someone the white of one's teeth with a smile than to feed a baby life sustaining milk. Frank always had a smile on his face and a good word to say about someone. If you felt down beforehand, you definitely felt better after speaking to him.

I personally experienced this in a very significant way.

At times, people can become overwhelmed by the vast number of *tzedakah* requests they receive. Even though we all know that *talmidei chachomim* are supposed to be treated with respect, one might become frustrated and temporarily forget this *halacha.* This might even unknowingly translate itself into behaving with a certain level of coarseness toward someone of great stature.

What people do not realize is that when they knock someone down, they are not just throwing out a comment. When a *rov* hears such a comment, he can lose impetus to collect for his organization. Unknowingly, a person might be causing damage to an entire *yeshiva.*

Not Frank Beda. He took every request with the greatest seriousness, and he looked at every contribution as a privilege to participate in the teaching of Torah to *Klal Yisroel*. Everyone left Frank's office with a good feeling that Frank really valued and appreciated the work that was being done.

One of the effects of the high-paced technology of this generation is that people have become almost mechanical in their conduct and look for speedy communication. It is difficult to speak to someone in a way that makes you feel that you are truly connected to that person. Frank immunized himself against this, and whenever we spoke, I felt that he was completely there with me.

Respecting Time

Frank was a person who cared about other people. He showed this daily in his personal interactions with his family and friends. I myself witnessed this on numerous occasions, especially on the *Shabbos* before last year *Pesach* which I spent in his home.

However, what made Frank stand out among others was the way he valued other people's time. He truly internalized what the *Chofetz Chaim* said regarding time being one of our most valuable assets. This concern about time expressed itself in many ways.

Frank valued the time of the *roshei yeshiva, roshei kollel,* and others who work for the benefit of *Klal Yisroel*. Rather than have them take of their time to come and visit him personally every year, he would send them contributions directly. If they called, he would tell them that he would be happy to meet them, but he did not want to take up their precious time.

Most people cannot fathom the extent of the kindness involved in this act. As a *rosh kollel*, I am well aware of the generally time-consuming task of collecting funds to run a *kollel*, and, at times, one gets so tired that he feels like he will collapse on his feet. That someone wants to spare one the effort involved shows sublime sensitivity.

Someone described Frank's acts of charity so succinctly: "A *tzaddik* who did all *mitzvos* behind closed doors, who donated so much money to worthy causes. We will miss you forever, but we will try and follow the amazing legacy that you left. Your words will always inspire me to strive to do better."

Frank's Final Requests

A few months before his passing, I spent *Shabbos* with Frank at his home in Flatbush. As we were walking to *shul*, he told me something surprising. He said, "What would happen if I would pass on from this world? I don't think that my family or I are ready for that." It was if his *neshamah* already sensed that his days in this world were numbered.

Shortly before his passing, at a wedding, Frank approached his cousin, Mrs. Sara Hadad, and asked her if her boys could act as big brothers for his children. She was surprised by what he said, but agreed. Only later did she realize the prophetic insight of his request.

Two weeks before his *petirah*, I called Frank about a project that we were working on together. He urged me to come to his summer home in Deal to learn with him. I told him that I would love to come but I did not think that I could fit such a trip into my schedule. *"The thoughts of man are many, but Hashem's will is fulfilled."* In the end, I traveled to Frank's home not to learn with Frank, but to deliver words of consolation to the family for the *shloshim*.

Frank is survived by his wife, Julie, and their six children, Moshe, Avraham, Yitzchak, Yaakov, Shlomo and Batya. In the merit of Frank's acts of kindness, may Hashem give his family strength to withstand the *nisyonos* of this trying time. May they experience true consolation together with the entire Jewish people, with the rebuilding of the *Bais Hamikdosh* and the return to Tzion.

Praying With Joy

A *beracha* for the continued health of

HaGaon Hatzadik
Harav Shlomo Brevda *shlita*

Who teaches how to "Pray With Joy"

From: Rabbi and Mrs. Akiva Aaronson. Rabbi and Mrs. Yonasan Alprin. Rabbi and Mrs. Elozar Barclay. Mr and Mrs. Frank Beda. Mr. David Bernstein. Mr. Richard Berry. Mr and Mrs. Dovid Collins. Rabbi and Mrs. Asher Eckstein. Rabbi and Mrs. Elchonan Fishman. Rabbi and Mrs. Shmuel Galandauer. Rabbi and Mrs. Nosson Gothold. Dr. and Mrs. David Eliezer Hirshman. Mr.and Mrs. Irving Laub. Mr and Mrs. Don Mishell. Rabbi and Mrs. Aryeh Kruskal. Rabbi and Mrs. Yaakov Lynn. Rabbi and Mrs. Avraham Marks. Reb and Mrs. Binyomin Moskovitz. Rabbi and Mrs. Yirmi Posen. Rabbi and Mrs. Pinchos Reisman. Mr. and Mrs. Yaakov Rosenblume. Rabbi and Mrs Yisroel Sander. Rabbi and Mrs. Mr. and Mrs. Michael Spiegel. Aryeh Leib Stern. Rabbi and Mrs. Ya'akov Tavin. Rabbi and Mrs. Daniel Travis. Rabbi and Mrs. Noach Umlas. Rabbi. and Mrs. Gershon Unger Mr. and Mrs. Naftoli Walfish. Mr. and Mrs. Donny Weinraub. Mr. and Mrs. Meir Weinraub.

RABBI S. BREVDA

שלמה ברעוודה

בעמח"ס להודות ולהלל, קימו וקבלו,
ליל שמורים, יבנה המקדש, ימי רצון,
עמלה של תורה
איפה שלמה על פי' הגר"א לשיר השירים,
יונה, תפלת חנה, חד גדיא

ראש חודש אדר ב' תשע"א

We are taught by our *Torah* teachers, that a person's repeated actions and deeds, eventually effect the deepest desires, beliefs, and aspirations of one's heart. *Emuna* – true belief in *Hashem Yisborach* as being the sole creator of the world, and since creation, the sole ruler of everything in the universe, and that He has given His *Torah* to His chosen people, the Jews, to be diligently studied and whose commandments should be fulfilled – the belief in these principles is called *Emuna*. The *Talmud* teaches us that *Emuna* is **the foundation** all 613 *Mitzvos*. The **slightest** flaw in *Emuna* has a profound effect on our entire practice of *Mitzvos*.

There is *Emuna* in **theory**, i.e. professing one's belief in *Hashem* and His *Torah*. And there is *Emuna* in practice, i.e. clinging steadfastly to *Hashem* and His *Torah's* laws in the face of **nisyonos**, situations full of temptations, financial and emotional.

Many words have been written and spoken, even today, to explain, to instill, and to strengthen *Emuna*. I humbly suggest, that **devout prayer** to Hashem, is the most powerful expression of **Emuna** **in practice** available to us daily, and is far more consequential in strengthening our *Emuna* than all of the talk about it!

It is, indeed, a source of true satisfaction to me, when reading that Rabbi Daniel Y. Travis came closer to devout prayer, through my advice to him at a time of acute *tzaros*. Since then, Rabbi Travis has embarked on an ambitious project, indeed, i.e. strengthening his own actions of prayer, and spreading the word to thousands of readers of his extremely well-written publications on prayer to *Hashem*.

Dear readers, permit me to add some words of clarification and inspiration concerning prayer to *Hashem*.

One may think: I pray three times a day, never miss a required prayer, and when I face a problem, I add a prayer to the end of *Shmone-Esrei*. What else do I have to learn about my attitude towards prayer (besides explanations of some words and their significance).

Dear readers, we still have a lot to learn about prayer. On example: Rabbeinu Yona *z'l* in his *peirush* on *Mishle* (10:28) teaches us an astonishing lesson about prayer. The *pasuk* says: The aspirations of *tzadikim* bring them joy, etc. Asks R. Yona, there is another *pasuk* which says (13:12) that aspiring for something for a long time, causes heartache.

R. Yona explains: when *tzadikim* hope and pray for something, they experience great joy over their prayers. They **never** base their hopes on their own strength and power, but rather upon the kindness of *Hashem*.

They never worry over the fact that they have been praying for many months for something, with no positive response from *Hashem* (realizing that *Hashem* knows **best** as to what is good for everyone). At the same time, they feel great satisfaction and joy over the fact that for a long period of time they have been putting their trust, hopes and aspirations **only** into a devout prayer to *Hashem* (and **not** into human initiative). And the more time that they spend on these prayers (weeks, months, with no positive response) the more joy and gratification they feel, knowing that these devout prayers are, indeed, actions of **great service** to *Hashem* by placing their hopes and faith only in Him.

Think into R. Yona's words. Are they not enlightening, to say the least! We all have quite a bit to learn about true prayer to *Hashem Yisborach*.

May *Hashem Yisborach* bless the endeavors of Rabbi Travis to strengthen true prayer amongst the Jewish People.

Sincerely,
Shlomo Brevda

שמואל קמנצקי

Rabbi S. Kamenetsky

2018 Upland Way
Philadelphia, Pa 19131

Home: 215-473-2798
Study: 215-473-1212

בס״ד כד׳ סיון תשס״ח

Kol hakavod to Rabbi Daniel Yaakov Travis, who has given us another outstanding *sefer*, this time on the subject of *tefillah*. Although this vital subject is one of the most important aspects of our lives and is critical to our *avodas Hashem*, people do not value it properly. ***Praying with Joy*** will surely help us appreciate our prayers and enhance and inspire our *tefillos*, helping them find favor in the Eyes of *Avinu Shebashamayim*.

May Rabbi Travis continue to be *mechazek* the *rabbim* with his works.

Rabbi S. Kamenetsky

RABBI YAAKOV PERLOW
1569 – 47TH STREET
BROOKLYN N.Y. 11219

יעקב פרלוב
קהל עדת יעקב נאוואמינסק
ישיבת נאוואמינסק – קול יהודא
ברוקלין. נ.י.

בס״ד
ז׳ ניסן תש״ע

Rabbi Daniel Yaakov Travis has written an illuminating and deep sefer on the meaning and depth of *Tefila*. In the structure of our time – consecrated prayers is given a new scope and analysis, halachically based, that will certainly enhance the *Avoda* of every committed Jew.

Praying With Joy is a significant contribution to our Torah heritage.

Table of Contents

Praying With Joy

Introduction

Complete Gratitude

The Gemara (*Brachos* 7b) writes: "Rav Yochanan said in the name of Rebbi Shimon bar Yochai: From the time that G-d created His world there was no one who thanked Him, until Leah Imeinu gave birth to Yehudah and expressed her gratitude, as the Torah writes, 'This time I will thank G-d'" (*Bereishis* 29:35). Although others had thanked G-d before her, Leah instituted a new mode of expressing appreciation that the others had not thought of. In order to understand her innovation, we must look at what preceded this act.

Yaakov Avinu was one of the most perfect individuals the world has known, so much so that our Sages say that his likeness is engraved on G-d's Throne of Glory. Yet after Lavan swindled him into marrying Leah instead of Rachel, Yaakov did not have the same feelings of affection for Leah as he had for Rachel. This distinction, as minute as it might have been, was felt by Leah on a significant scale.

The Torah writes that because of this slight difference in Yaakov's feelings for his two wives, Leah experienced tremendous anguish; so much so that in naming each of her first three sons Leah described her pain and incorporated this feeling into their names. By the time her fourth son, Yehudah, was born, however, she no longer mentioned her negative feelings; instead she thanked G-d joyfully. What caused this change?

At the time Leah married Yaakov, she was incapable of having children. The Torah writes, "G-d saw that Leah was not loved as much as Rachel, and He opened her womb" (*Bereishis* 29:31). G-d took Leah's suffering into account, and therefore not only did He make her fertile, He also caused her to bear sons before Yaakov Avinu's other wives did (Seforno).

All of the Matriarchs were prophets, and they knew that there were to be twelve Tribes. Thus it was reasonable for them to assume that each of Yaakov's four wives was entitled to have three sons. When Leah's fourth son was born, she recognized that the pain she had endured as a result of being "second choice" had paid off, for she had merited having an extra child as a result.

At that moment, her anguish turned to joy, and in retrospect she thanked G-d not only for the birth of Yehudah, but also for having placed her in a position where she would merit having additional children. Not only did she stop mentioning that Yaakov did not love her as much as Rachel, she expressed gratitude to G-d in a grand way that had never been done before: she expressed her thanks for a good that had originally seemed bad. This attitude was later incorporated into the halachah, as the *Shulchan Aruch* writes, "A person should always accustom himself to saying that whatever G-d does is for good" (*Shulchan Aruch, Orach Chaim* 230:5).

It is clear that we should also try to follow Leah's path in our relationship to G-d. Divine ways are beyond our understanding, and we never really know what the outcome of any event will be. Establishing in our own minds what is "good" and what is "bad" shows a certain lack of gratitude to G-d, Who is constantly watching over each of us every second of the day to ensure that whatever happens is the best for us.

This is what the Gemara (*Brachos* 7b) means when it writes that Leah was the first to thank Hashem. Certainly others had thanked Hashem beforehand, but Leah initiated thanking Hashem for the bad as well as the good. Trying to see the good within the bad, and recognizing that everything that Hashem does is good even if we do not understand it, is real *hodayah*.

In this light it is understandable why, in the Gemara cited above, it was Rabbi Shimon bar Yochai who made this comment about Leah. Rabbi Shimon was sentenced to death by the Romans and was forced to hide in a cave for thirteen years. We might think that this was a tremendous personal and national tragedy. However, Rabbi Shimon himself said later that it was only because of those years he spent in hiding that he was able to reach such a deep and thorough understanding of the Torah (*Shabbos* 33b).

Shiva after *Sheva*

After I was engaged to marry my wife, both of us anxiously awaited the date of our wedding. What a shock it was to hear on Tisha B'Av, four days before the scheduled date of our wedding, that my prospective father-in-law had passed away! According to halacha a mourner must wait a month before getting married, and it seemed as if we would have to put off the wedding.

Our *mesader kiddushin*, Rav Moshe Meiselman, took me to consult with Rav Shlomo Zalman Auerbach, *zt"l*. Rav Shlomo Zalman heard the story and calmly replied that we should not tell my future wife that her father had passed away. This way, she would not become a mourner, and we would be able to get married as planned.

My father-in-law had been living in Rio de Janeiro, Brazil, and had been suffering from cancer before the wedding. My wife realized that he might not be attending the wedding, but she was still surprised that neither he nor her mother even called her beforehand. My mother-in-law accepted the ruling of Rav Auerbach, and did not speak to my wife about the matter.

The wedding went ahead as planned, and by the time the date arrived most of our guests knew that my father-in-law was no longer with us. Eyes were filled with tears, and my wife assumed that they were tears of joy. Little did she suspect the real reason behind these tears.

A week after the wedding, after seven consecutive nights of rejoicing that accompany a Jewish wedding, one of my wife's teachers broke the news to her that she would now start the seven days of mourning over the death of her father. She was startled, but accepted the ruling of the great Rav Shlomo Zalman.

How ironic it was to see the same faces that we had seen for the past seven days of rejoicing returning to offer consolation to my wife. Everyone was very kind and listened as my wife poured out her heart about her father. At the end of seven days we got on a plane and for the first time I made the trip to Brazil to meet my mother-in-law in Rio de Janeiro.

A Year of *Tzaros*

One morning while we were in Brazil, I went down to the beach in order to be *tovel* in the sea, and I was attacked by two bandits. One of them forced my head into the sand while choking me, while the other one looked through my belongings. I vividly remember how he kept repeating, "No money, *amigo* [my friend], no money?"

For almost two minutes I was without oxygen and really thought that the end had come. My life passed in front of my eyes as everything started to slow down. However, as quickly as they came they suddenly left.

We returned from Brazil and rented a small apartment in Jerusalem. The first holiday that my wife and I spent together was Sukkos, and I spent three days building a sukkah in the small plot of land next to our apartment. My wife was expecting and she was too sick to cook, so I went into the city to get food for the holiday.

When I returned home an hour before the start of the holiday I was shocked to see the sukkah that I had constructed was lying smashed on the ground. The neighbor explained to me that in the course of building the sukkah I had stepped on some of her husband's flowers. Enraged at the audacity of such an act, he destroyed the sukkah.

We decided that we were not welcome in that neighborhood and purchased an apartment in another part of Jerusalem. The previous owners could not move out immediately, and in the interim we rented an apartment in another part of Jerusalem. That winter was one of the coldest and snowiest in Jerusalem history, and unfortunately the heating system broke down, and the walls were not properly insulated. We spent two months freezing, trying our best to keep warm with small electric heaters.

Finally we moved into our apartment, but quickly realized that we would not be able to stay in that neighborhood. Unfortunately, when we tried to sell the apartment we found out that we did not legally own the apartment. Nobody would buy an illegal apartment, and we were stuck there for another year until we could straighten out the situation.

Meanwhile, our daughter, Nechama Rachel, was born. Four weeks after I was on the way to buy food for a *kiddush* in honor of our newborn daughter, and the next thing I remember was waking up on a stretcher being wheeled into Hadassah Hospital in Ein Kerem. Bewildered and in pain, I was astonished to hear that I had been in a serious car accident. An experienced medical technician who "happened" to witness the accident began to care for me immediately and called an ambulance to the scene.

The neurologist told my wife that after I had landed headfirst from a three-meter fall onto the concrete, she should expect that I would be permanently brain damaged. To the amazement of the neurologist and the rest of the medical staff, however, tests showed that I had suffered no major physical or neurological damage. The neurologist said that although he did not believe in Hashem, there was no way to explain what had happened other than saying that a miracle had taken place.

Unwilling to give up so easily, the doctors sent me from ward to ward checking for some permanent damage that had transpired as a result of the accident. I had scratches on my eyes and was told that if they had been a drop higher I would be blind. In each ward the doctors admitted that a miracle had taken place. After three days of checking, they sent me home.

After the accident I met up with someone and told him what had happened. His face turned white, and I asked him what was wrong. He told me that David Hamelech had foreseen what would happen to me. King David wrote, "How precious is Your kindness, Hashem! The sons of man take refuge in the shadow of Your wings" (*Tehillim* 36:8). The Hebrew word for "take refuge" is spelled *yud, ches, samech, yud, vav, nun* — spelling out 18 Sivan, the date of my accident — a clear indication that "*chai*" Sivan is a special day of Divine protection.

I recovered quickly from the accident, and within a month I was able to walk on crutches. Our apartment was downstairs, and one time I slipped on the steps and fell down the stairs. I was taken to the hospital but sustained no major injury.

A short time after I recovered from the accident, I was studying in a yeshiva near our home. Suddenly, a young boy ran into the room and told me that my house was on fire. I quickly ran home to find ambulances and fire trucks at the scene. Once again, we were rushed to the hospital.

My wife told me that the small floor heater had exploded while she and the baby were sleeping. When she woke up for a moment, she noticed that the house was very dark, and then became aware of the fire. They were treated for smoke inhalation, and we were released on Friday night.

Searching for Salvation

Day after day these *tzaros* continued, and my wife and I felt that we must have a very bad *mazal*. I checked our mezuzos and tefillin, but they were kosher. Someone pointed out that the first letters of our names (Daniel Yaakov and Nomi) spell *din,* and maybe we needed to change our names. However, I went to Rav Yisrael Yaakov Fisher, *zt"l,* and he said that our names were fine. He suggested my wife wear an amulet around her neck, but this did not produce any significant change in our situation.

Unable to cope with all of these *tzaros*, we turned to other Rabbanim for direction. Rav Shlomo Brevda assured me that the only possible solution when one is undergoing such an extraordinary number of *tsaros* is *tefillah*. He urged me to plead with Hashem for help at the end of the *Shemoneh Esrei* of *Shacharis* and *Mincha*, before taking three steps backward, and to conclude my petition with the following prayer:

"Even though I am not worthy to ask for such requests, nonetheless please do not leave me empty-handed before You, for I am pleading to You with a broken heart, and on Your tremendous kindness and Your incredible mercy I put all of my trust, may my heart rejoice in Your salvation."

אף על פי שאיני כדאי לבקש בקשות כאלו, מכל מקום נא אל תשיבני ריקם מלפניך, כי בלב נשבר הנני מתחנן מלפניך, ועל גודל טובך ורחמיך העצומים הנני בוטח ונשען, יגל ליבי בישועתך.

Rav Brevda told me, in the name of his rebbe, Rav Yechezkel Levenstein, that most people think that when they have *tzaros* they should pray in order to get away from them. But troubles are the "illness" and *tefillah* is the "cure." Hashem brings us *tzaros* because He wants to hear our prayers. Rav Brevda's words of *chizuk* touched me deeply, and soon after I began to recite this *tefillah* regularly during *Shacharis* and *Mincha*, our situation improved radically.

Good from Bad

On the first anniversary of my accident, on 18 Sivan, I made a *seudas hodayah* in yeshiva. After I spoke, I realized that although I had come close to death and been saved miraculously, I had not made any significant changes in my life. Something seemed wrong, and I consulted with Rabbanim about what I should do. They answered that if Hashem had saved my life He surely expected something from me, but only I could know what that was. I turned to Hashem in *tefillah* for guidance.

I started to research the halachos regarding the blessing one makes upon revisiting a place where one had experienced a miracle. As a result of this study, I soon had a manuscript on these halachos ready to publish. Someone suggested to me that I combine the text with Torah insights from great rabbanim, and almost miraculously I had soon collected two hundred pages of these writings and was able to publish them, together with an analysis of the halachos on *birkas hodayah*, under the title *Mizmor Lesodah*, my "song of thanks" in book form.

Mizmor Lesodah was my first serious undertaking in the learning of halachah, and I found it a gratifying experience. I joined Kollel La'asukei Shemaisa, under the guidance of Rabbi Yitzchak Kaufman, *shlita*, and studied in-depth halachic topics on an advanced level. We learned the laws of kashrus and published a second *sefer*, *Yoreh Binah*, an encyclopedia of the concepts of kashrus.

Although the *tzaros* had certainly let up, they continued to come on a fairly regular basis. One day I came home from yeshiva with a bad headache, which got worse and worse through the night. In the morning I could hardly move, and I was rushed to the hospital. I was diagnosed with meningitis, a potentially fatal illness.

I was given very strong antibiotics and *b'chasdei Shamayim* recovered. However, I was so weakened from the medicines that a few months later I contracted pneumonia. It seemed like our *tzaros* were back, and I wondered what else I could do to get away from them.

One Friday night I was learning with a *chavrusa*, and we came across the Gemara at the end of *Brachos* that if someone wakes up with a *passuk* on his lips it is a *nevua katana*, a small prophecy. I davened to Hashem that He should give us insight into our situation, and sure enough woke up with a *passuk* on my lips, "*Va'yehi b'yeshurun melech.*"

I saw Rav Hirsch's explanation that Yeshurun is a name for the Jewish people when they act with *yashrus*, and began to study the halachos connected to *yashrus*. Eventually this became an English *sefer*, *Priceless Integrity*.

After I wrote this *sefer*, my editor suggested that I should write for the English Torah newspapers. I started doing so, and the articles eventually became *sefarim*. I published four more *sefarim* in English and merited to publish *Mizmor Lesodah* three more times.

After seven years in Kollel La'asukei Shemaisa, I felt a need to give over to others that which I had acquired, and with tremendous help from Above I launched my own halacha *kollel*. I decided to call the program "Toras Chaim" ("The Torah of Life"), in an attempt to express my infinite gratitude to G-d for all of the kindness He has bestowed on me in keeping me alive so that I may serve Him.

Since my accident, I have recounted my story many times, with the following addition. My close friend Rav Ben Zion Kermaier was at the site of the accident, and someone told him that I had been killed. If you had asked him at that moment whether something good or bad had just taken place, he would probably have said, "What a great tragedy. A young *avreich* just passed away four weeks after his first child was born!"

However, when reflecting on all that has transpired from the time of the accident until today, I realized that had it not been for the all of the seeming "misfortunes," I probably would not have involved myself in these projects. I have learned to appreciate that the very things that seem worst are actually G-d's way of meting out tremendous benevolence to us.

This Time I Thank Hashem

B'chasdei Shamayim, "Praying With Joy" is my eighth published work after my accident. As Leah said after her fourth child, "*Hapa'am odeh es Hashem*," I can sincerely thank Him for giving me much more than my portion. My deepest desire is that Hashem should continue to bestow His infinite kindness upon my family and me, and always help us to see the good in everything He does.

I am especially grateful to my friend Jerry Balsam for helping me with this work. In addition to helping to finance and edit the book, he was a constant source of encouragement and positive feedback. May this work be a source of merit to his late wife, Joy (Rochwarger) Balsam, to whom this work is dedicated.

I must also thank Joy's brother Geoff, as well as Andy Lowinger and Morris Smith, as well as all of the generous individuals who helped finance this project. May the merit of Torah be a source of great blessing for them and their families.

I cannot begin to express the incredible appreciation that my wife and I have to all of our Rabbanim for their continual support, advice and direction in all aspects of our lives, especially Rav Shlomo Brevda, Rav Elchanan Fishman, Rav Ben Zion Kermaier, Rav Yitzchak Kaufman and Rav Yirmiyahu Kaganoff. May they all be blessed with many years of health and peace of mind in order to continue publicly sanctifying Hashem's Name. Through their *mesiras nefesh*, constant *ameilus beTorah, dikduk beHalacha*, guidance of *talmidim*, and extraordinary *shiurim* in all areas of Torah, they are an example to us all.

I owe tremendous gratitude to Rav Nachman Bulman, *zt"l*, who had a profound influence on me and many members of our community during his Rabbanus of Beis Knesses Nachliel. May this *sefer* be a *nachas ruach* to his *neshama*, and serve as testimony to the legacy he left behind in the form of his *talmidim*.

I thank my parents, Mr. Philip and Mrs. Nancy Travis, and my mother-in-law, Mrs. Sara Kerstenetzky, whose love and kindness is exceeded only by their good nature; and to all of my teachers who gave me the tools to acquire this world and the World to Come.

I must also express my appreciation to all of my *talmidim* in Kollel Toras Chaim, as well as Rav Eliezer Barclay, N. Elbinger, M. Jakubowicz, who helped check, edit and proofread this book, F. Savitsky who did a beautiful job laying out this book, to *hayakar shebeyekarim*, my brother, Rav Binyamin, *moreh tzedek* in Cincinnati, Ohio, and his wife, Elisa; and *acharon acharon chaviv*, my wife, Nomi, and our children, Nechamah Rachel and Chaim Yitzchak, who are a constant source of warmth and *nachas*. May Hashem shower *bracha* upon them and bring them only health, happiness, and true success.

Rabbi Daniel Yaakov Travis
Sivan, 5768 - *Jerusalem, Israel*

Everyone goes through difficult times in life. I remember
...riencing crises, and reaching the point where I couldn't bear
...anymore. During those moments I reached into the depths of my
...t, and turned to Hashem in sincere prayer. As I said the words I
...that my tefilos were bokeah shemayim, that they had ripped open
...heavens, and not long afterwards I experienced salvation.

Ripping Open the Heavens

...metimes I feel	You call me beloved
...st can't go on	And beckon me onwards
...much to carry	Hastening redemption
...much to bear	As only You can
...ing these tests	I respond to the call
...pain is great	And look for Your kindness
...the farther I get	Soul searching
...sharper the sting	For something gone wrong
...heart screams	Please give me strength
...my body is numb	To feel salvation
...in my mind	Unwavering faith
...ow You are one	In the face of Your trials
...hat very moment	Prayers from within
...lift me up	To rip open the heavens
...ry my burden	Show me Your mercy
...ring my pain	To laugh in the end

About This Book

"Praying With Joy" is divided into twenty-four chapters; each chapter addresses one section of the morning *tefillos*.

Every chapter comprises seven short sections, one for each day of the week, so the reader will be able to internalize and retain the concepts presented. The chapters explore the *tefillos* through stories, halachos, and related *mussar-*concepts, allowing us to penetrate beyond the surface level of the words we are saying and to experience the depth of conversing with Hashem.

May "Praying With Joy" help inspire and enhance our daily prayers!

1

Waking Up Jewish

Understanding the Halachos
of Getting Out of Bed

Early to Rise | SHABBOS

It was a momentous and joyous occasion when two of our era's greatest rabbis, Rav Yosef Shalom Eliyashiv and Rav Shlomo Zalman Auerbach, celebrated the marriage of their children. However, the reception was barely underway when Rav Shlomo Zalman noticed Rav Eliyashiv put on his coat and get ready to leave. Surprised, Rav Auerbach asked him where he was going.

"You know that one of my primary learning sessions is in the early hours of the morning," Rav Eliyashiv replied. "For many years I have gone to sleep at 10 p.m. and woken up at 2 a.m. If I don't leave now I will not be able to get up for my regular morning Torah study."

"Rav Yosef Shalom," Rav Shlomo Zalman responded, "I believe that in this instance you must make an exception. I hereby rule that you are obligated to stay until the end of this wedding."

In memory of Alvin Stahler
An outstanding, dedicated and loving father and grandfather.
He truly was a model of Praying With Joy. From Ushi and Esti Stahler and Family.

Rav Eliyashiv accepted this ruling, took off his coat, and continued rejoicing until late into the night.

Many Torah scholars throughout the ages have made it their practice to go to bed early and wake up to learn in the predawn hours. One important commentator, the Kaf HaChaim, writes that one hour of learning before dawn is equal to many hours of learning during the day (1,24). Nonetheless, the Rambam indicates that it is preferable to stay up late and learn during the night (*Dei'os* 4,4). Other authorities support this view and encourage going to sleep after midnight (*Arugas HaBosem* 1).

While giving serious consideration to what the Torah greats say about waking up and going to sleep, there is another critical factor that must be taken into account. Each person should honestly evaluate how much sleep he needs and when his energy levels are at their peak, and take these into consideration when deciding when to go to sleep and wake up. Whatever one chooses to do, it is crucial to remember these wise words: "It is better to sleep well at night than to cut back on sleep and be tired all day" (*Taz, Even HaEzer* 25,1).

Modeh Ani | SUNDAY

"I admit [*Modeh ani*] before You [Hashem] the living and everlasting King, that You returned my soul with mercy, great is Your faithfulness!" The first thing a Jew should do when he opens his eyes in the morning is acknowledge that Hashem has returned his soul to him. He accomplishes this by reciting the prayer *Modeh Ani* as soon as he wakes up in the morning.

Our Sages tell us that the experience of sleep is one-sixtieth of death (*Brachos 57b*). For this reason, King David was careful to minimize his sleep so he should not "taste the flavor of death" (*Shulchan Aruch* 4,16 citing *Zohar Vayigash* 207a). Towards the end of his life, the Vilna Gaon acted in a similar fashion, never sleeping for the amount of time that is considered one-sixtieth of death, which is more than half an hour according to most opinions.

Every morning when we wake up, we are resurrected from the semi-death experience of sleep. By referring to Hashem as "the Everlasting King," we remind ourselves of this fundamental principle of Jewish faith. We affirm that just as we have been given our life anew in this world, so too at the End of Days all of the dead will be resurrected by the Everlasting King.

Most prayers may not be recited if one's hands have touched parts of the body that are generally covered. In a case where one is unsure, such as after a night's sleep, the hands must be washed first. Nevertheless, we may recite *Modeh Ani* immediately upon waking, since it does not contain any of Hashem's Names (*Mishna Berura* 1,8).

When a person dies, the soul leaves the body, rendering it impure. Sleep is like death, and while a person is asleep, a similar type of impure spirit (*ruach ra'ah*) descends on his hands. He should wash his hands as soon as possible, to remove this impure spirit.

Most authorities agree that one recites a blessing of *al netilas yadayim* only when the washing is a mitzva, e.g. washing for bread. Washing away an impure spirit is only a protective measure and not a mitzva (*Pri Migadim, Eshel Avraham* 4,1; *Mishna Berura* 4,8). Why, then, do we say a blessing after we wash our hands in the morning?

Some early commentators connect this washing to the renewal of our life force each morning. Just as a *kohen* had a mitzva to purify himself before starting his service in the Temple, we also have a mitzva to wash our hands each morning to start a new day of Divine service (*Responsa of Rashba* 1,191).

Others write that there is a mitzva to wash our hands before each regular prayer, in case we had touched a place on the body that is generally covered (*Responsa of Rosh* 4,1). Since this act is considered to have the status of a mitzva, we therefore recite a blessing. These two reasons give the washing the status of a mitzva and are sufficient to obligate making a blessing on the washing.

The halacha rules that one should wash his right hand first. The Zohar explains the deeper meaning of this practice. "A person should wash his right hand with his left, in order that the right [representing kindness] should overpower the left [representing justice]" (*Vayeshev* 184b).

However, in another section, the *Zohar* tells us: "The water for *netilas yadayim* should be taken with one's right hand" (*Teruma* 154b). If the water is in the right hand, then the implication is that the left hand should be washed first. How can we understand this seeming contradiction?

These two passages are practically reconciled as follows: First, the cup of water is taken in the right hand, then it is passed to the left hand, showing that kindness (represented by the right hand) overpowers justice (represented by the left hand) (*Shulchan Aruch* 4,10). Washing the right hand first further demonstrates the superiority of kindness over justice (*Mishna Berura* 4,21). This simple action helps ensure that the attribute of Hashem's kindness will be showered on us throughout the forthcoming day. (The application of this halacha is the same even if one is left-handed.)

Created with Wisdom |

"From my flesh I see G-d" (*Job* 19,26). Contemplating the innumerable complex and miraculous functions that the human body faithfully performs every second of the day elevates us to a state of awe and wonder. Our Sages gave us the opportunity to express this feeling on a constant basis while reciting the blessing of *asher yatzar* after visiting the restroom.

Ideally, *asher yatzar* should be recited as soon as one washes his hands after leaving the restroom. However, if it was delayed, the blessing can still be recited. If one has waited so long that he already needs to return to the restroom, he may not say *asher yatzar* until he leaves (*Mishna Berura* 7,1).

Often, *asher yatzar* is recited at a time when one is rushing to get back to business. During these instances, we should try to keep in mind that while conversing with Hashem we should not be involved with any other activity (*Makor Chaim* 4,1). Even Torah learning is forbidden while reciting a blessing (*Mishna Berura* 191,5).

Returning Our Souls |

As mentioned previously, when we go to sleep our souls leave our bodies. As soon as we wake up in the morning, they are returned to us, rejuvenated for a new day. Therefore, right after saying *asher yatzar*, which acknowledges the gift of our bodily functions, we thank Hashem for implanting in us a Divine spark, our soul, and returning it to us today.

Unlike the other morning blessings, the *Elokai neshama* blessing does not start with the word "*baruch*." Some halachic authorities explain that this blessing does not need to start with *baruch*, while others rule that it should be said following another blessing so that the *baruch* of that blessing will be adjacent to *Elokai neshama*. One should try to follow the latter opinion and say *Elokai neshama* immediately after *asher yatzar*.

Let's look at the example of Aharon, who overslept one morning. When he noticed the time he jumped out of bed and ran to shul. In his hurry, he forgot to say *Elokai neshama* before reciting the other prayers.

According to some views, acknowledgment for the return of our souls in the morning is covered by the blessing of resurrection of the dead, which is part of the *Shemoneh Esrei*. Since the halacha can be extremely complex, Aharon should consult with a rabbi on whether he may recite *Elokai neshama* after he has completed all the other prayers (*Mishna Berura* 6,12; *Biur Halacha* 52,1).

Like a Lion |

"Arise like a lion to serve your Creator in the morning" (*Shulchan Aruch* 1,1). As Jews, we are taught that if we have the mindset of a lion, we will successfully overcome the challenge of getting ourselves out of bed in the morning. What is the significance of this analogy?

Over two thousand years ago, our Sages recognized that the urge to worship idols was too powerful for the Jewish people to resist, and they prayed that it should be removed. Hashem complied and a fire-like lion ascended from the Holy of Holies. Our Sages captured this negative inclination (*yetzer hara)*, preventing it from having further influence (*Yuma* 69).

From this Talmudic story, we see that the negative inclination takes the form of a lion. Strategically speaking, if we want to defeat it, we must also act like lions. For this reason, the *Shulchan Aruch* advises us to start our day like a lion (*ibid. Shaarei Teshuva* 1,1).

Lions are unique in the animal kingdom in that they fear nothing. Even an armed man, who is more dangerous than a lion, does not arouse fear in this majestic creature.

When confronting the *yetzer hara*, we must employ similar tactics. Even though the negative inclination is stronger than man, we must fight it with all our might, turning to Hashem to aid us in this struggle and never fearing defeat. In this way, we will win the battle (*Taz* 1,1).

Waking up in the morning is the first battle of the day. Generally, as soon as the alarm clock rings, we immediately think of many reasons why we should stay in bed a few minutes longer. It is at this moment that we must become lion-like, pushing away the cunning arguments of the negative inclination and escaping from his grip – and from the lures of sleepiness.

Getting out of bed
is our first challenge of the day.
The first tefillos of the day aid us to be
victorious in this battle.

2

Learning with Joy

Understanding Birkas HaTorah

Simchas Torah | SHABBOS

Rav Aharon Kotler was a Torah giant and one of the foremost pioneers of Torah in America. His students listened to his words with thirst, and he directed many Torah luminaries on their paths to greatness. Although Rav Aharon had many outstanding character traits, there is one that his students particularly remember.

Whenever Rav Kotler said the word *"Torah,"* his entire being would light up. Just the mention of this word elevated him to a state of jubilation. His students would purposely try to get him to say the word *Torah* in order to see his elation.

When Rav Baruch Ber Leibowitz gave a Torah class, he was elevated to great heights of joy. His students recalled that seeing him give a class was like watching someone dining at a tasty gourmet meal. Torah was the greatest pleasure of his life.

When Rav Chaim Brisker was a young student, there was a gathering of Rabbanim in Europe to hear his first Talmudic

In memory of
HaRav Avraham Yaakov Halevi ben Moshe Ginsberg

discourse. He spoke on the topic of *"heilich,"* (Bava Metzia 4a) one of the most complicated sections of the Talmud. Afterwards the rabbis were so happy that the next generation had been blessed with such a *gaon*, that they all danced in a circle in the *beis medrash*.

Most of us are not on the level of these Torah luminaries, but we also enjoy Torah learning according to our personal levels. In addition to the happiness of studying Torah, the halacha says that the blessing on Torah should be recited with great joy (*Mishna Berura* 47,2). Let us investigate its halachos, so that we can express our joy about Torah learning.

Double Blessing | SUNDAY

According to the Sephardim, the first blessing on the Torah is, "Who commanded us on words of Torah" (*Shulchan Aruch* 47,5). Why don't Ashkenazim mention Torah learning in the blessing? By saying a more general wording we also thank Hashem for the opportunity to perform His mitzvos that are written in the Torah (*Abudaraham*).

The custom among Ashkenazim is to say, "...to involve ourselves in the words of Torah." According to this understanding, since we make a separate blessing before doing each mitzva, there is no need to mention that we are learning Torah to be able to perform other mitzvos (*Beis Yosef*). We focus specifically on the mitzva to learn Torah, and to completely involve ourselves in it.

After the first blessing, both Ashkenazim and Sephardim say another blessing, "*veha'arev na*" - "please make the Torah sweet" - asking Hashem to ensure that our Torah learning is enjoyable. Most halachic authorities say that the blessing begins with the word *and*, for it is a continuation of the previous blessing. Since they are a single blessing, many authorities rule not to answer *amen* between them. Therefore, if others are listening it is proper to say the first blessing silently so they should not have to answer *amen* (*Mishna Berura* 47,12).

Praying for Children | MONDAY

In the blessing of "*veha'arev na*" we ask that our offspring should be Torah scholars. Since our Sages promise that if the Torah stays with us for three generations it will never leave, some add a request that our grandchildren should also be Talmudic scholars (*Elia Rabba* 47,3). Others rule that we only need to mention offspring, which includes all subsequent generations (*Mishna Berura* 47,9).

When asking for the success of our offspring in Torah, we should have special concentration in order that our prayers should be answered. Similarly, when saying the blessing of "*ahava rabba*" (abundant love) before *Shema*, and the words "so we do not struggle in vain or produce for futility" in the *uva l'Tzion* prayer, we should think about our children, since these words refer to them.

The Chasam Sofer had many generations of Torah scholars as descendants. When asked what his secret was, he pointed to his hat. "More than once I filled this hat up with tears while praying that my offspring should devote themselves to Torah," he said. Meriting offspring who are Talmudic scholars requires constant prayers (*Mishna Berura* 47: 9-10).

The Chosen Nation | TUESDAY

After "*veha'arev na*" we make another blessing, "Who chose us from among the nations to give us His Torah." Most mitzvos only require one blessing. What is the nature of this additional blessing?

Aside from the mitzva of studying Torah, there is another aspect of Torah we must recognize with a blessing. If it were not for the Torah, we would be just like all of the other nations of the world. Every day we thank Hashem for elevating us with the gift of His Torah (*Igros Moshe, Orach Chaim* 3,2).

The blessing of "*asher bachar banu*" is also recited when someone is called up for an *aliya* to the Torah. If a person was unable to say the blessings on the Torah before shul and then received an *aliya*, since he already said "*asher bachar banu*" as part of his *aliya* he need not repeat it afterwards (*Mishna Berura* 139: 31,32).

Torah Readings | WEDNESDAY

Every morning we recite blessings before learning Torah. When a man is called up to the Torah he repeats the blessing of "*asher bachar banu*" and afterwards says, "*asher nasan lanu.*" Why does he need to say these two blessings if he has already recited blessings on the Torah?

Moshe Rabbeinu instituted a special mitzva to read publicly from the Torah every Shabbos. Ezra Hasofer added that the Torah be read on Monday, Thursday and Shabbos afternoon to ensure that no Jew should pass three days without Torah learning. Since the public Torah reading is a specially instituted decree, we recite independent blessings on it (*Responsa of Rashba*; *Rosh Brachos* 1,13).

Every person who reads from the Torah makes a blessing afterwards as well. In truth, we are instructed to learn Torah day and night, and it is really not possible to recite an "after blessing" on Torah learning. This blessing merely marks the conclusion of one's *aliya* to the Torah (*Beis Yosef* 47).

Thinking and Writing |

"…and he thinks about His Torah day and night" (*Yehoshua* 1,8). From here the Vilna Gaon derives that one must recite a blessing before thinking about Torah. Both the *Shulchan Aruch* and Rema disagree, and do not require a blessing to think about Torah (47,4).

When performing a mitzva, one will inevitably have to think about the halachos connected to its execution. Even according to the Vilna Gaon, who requires a blessing to think about Torah, one can do a mitzva without first reciting the blessings on the Torah. Since one's intention is not to learn but to perform the mitzva properly, no blessing is required (*Mishna Berura* 47,7).

Writing differs from thinking in that it is more of a physical action, and at times a person speaks as he writes. Because of this the *Shulchan Aruch* rules that one should make a blessing when writing words of Torah. However, most authorities equate writing with thinking, and do not require a blessing (*Mishna Berura* 47,4).

If someone wakes up early in the morning to write tefillin and mezuzos, must he recite the blessing on the Torah beforehand? When writing professionally, a person may not be required to recite the blessings on Torah beforehand. Therefore, he should make sure to learn Torah after saying the blessings on Torah, before he starts to write (*Biur Halacha* 47,3).

"Torah has the power to protect those who study it, yet the Land of Israel was destroyed [during the time of the destruction of the Temple]. Why didn't the Torah study guard the Jewish people? This question was posed to the Sages, to the Prophets, and the heavenly Servants, and no one could answer. Finally Hashem answered this question: Although the Jewish people were studying Torah, in essence they abandoned it when they failed to recite the blessing on the Torah at the first opportunity" (*Nedarim* 81a).

The Talmud specifies that this severe punishment was meted out because the Jewish people did not recite the blessing first. This implies that they did say the blessings on the Torah, but that there was a problem with their recitation. They did not say it at the first possible opportunity in order that they should not pass even the shortest time unable to learn Torah.

Torah is more than another branch of knowledge; it is the life-sustaining force of a Jew. When studying Torah, it should be with an excitement and zest that Torah is the focal point of our lives. We give expression to this feeling by reciting the blessings on Torah as soon as we wake up.

Torah distinguishes us from all other nations.

The blessings on Torah help us to appreciate our exclusive status.

3

Appreciating Gifts

Understanding the Morning Blessings

It's Good to Be a Jew | SHABBOS

A number of years ago a non-Jew came to Yerushalayim. He had come to the conclusion, following a long spiritual search, that he wanted to convert to Judaism. He underwent the normal process of rigorous study and testing in the hope that he would be accepted. One day, the *beis din* contacted him with a positive answer, and he immediately underwent all the procedures necessary to convert.

The following day his neighbors woke up to a very peculiar sight. That very same convert was seen dancing through the streets of Yerushalayim singing, "*Shelo asani goy, shelo asani goy* [thanking Hashem for not creating him as a member of the other nations of the world]!"

When members of the *beis din* found out about this, they thought that perhaps he was mentally unstable and wanted to reconsider the validity of the conversion. However, Rav

L'zecher Nishmas
Shlomo Zev ben Baruch Yehuda Nutovic

David Baharan, an elderly Torah scholar on the *beis din* of Yerushalayim, stopped them.

"No, no," he said. "This man is not disturbed, and there should be no question of revoking the conversion. That is really the way we should all recite the blessing of *shelo asani goy!*"

In practice, since a convert was not born Jewish, the Rema rules he cannot say, "I was not made a goy," and he therefore does not recite the blessing "*shelo asani goy.*" He can express his thanks to Hashem and say, "Who made me a convert" (*Rema* 46,4).

The Zohar, however, explains that every night our souls ascend to heaven to be recharged and cleansed for the upcoming day. During this time the possibility exists of *ibur neshama*, that our soul could come back down to this world with another soul attached to it. Therefore, even a convert can thank Hashem that when He returned his now Jewish soul, He did not send with it the soul of a non-Jew (*Magen Avraham* 46,9).

Let us investigate the halachos of this blessing and the other morning blessings, in order that we may understand their deeper meaning.

Almost all of the morning blessings are in the positive, except for three: "Who did not create me [a member of the] other nations of the world"; "Who did not make me a slave"; and (for men) "Who did not make me a woman." Why are these blessings phrased negatively?

Our Sages saw fit to establish three separate blessings to give us the opportunity to express our appreciation for every facet of Hashem's kindness. If I would simply thank the One "Who made me a Jew," thanking Hashem for not making me a slave or a woman as well would seem superfluous. Additionally, we should not say the blessings in reverse order, for the last blessing implies the praise of the first two. Saying these blessings in the negative allows us to recite all three blessings, thus increasing our praise of our Creator (*Mishna Berura* 46,15).

Some *siddurim* cite this blessing with alternative wording: "Who did not make me an idol worshipper." Although we are certainly thankful for not practicing idolatry, our gratitude goes beyond this base level. We say, "did not create me as a member [of] the other nations of the world" in order to express that we are happy that we were given the Torah and elevated above all of the nations (*Responsa Teshuvos V'hanhagos* 1,6).

Out of Order

Getting out of bed in the morning is generally a two-step process. After we wake up, we stretch out on the bed in order to break the bonds of sleep from our muscles. We thank Hashem for this capability when reciting the blessing *matir assurim*, "Who frees the imprisoned."

After we have woken up sufficiently to get out of bed, we stand up and straighten ourselves. This removes us completely from the world of sleep. We thank Hashem for this action when reciting *zokef kefufim*, "Who straightens the bent."

Although the order of most of the morning blessings is not exact, we should make sure to recite these two in order (*Shulchan Aruch* 46,5). After we have thanked Hashem for straightening the bent, we may no longer thank Him for freeing us from the shackles of sleep when we initially woke up. If we erroneously recite *zokef kefufim* before *matir assurim*, we should hear *matir assurim* from someone else and answer *amen* (*Mishna Berura* 46,20).

According to some opinions, the same rule holds true for the three *brachos* of *shelo asani goy*, *eved* and *isha* (Who did not me create me as a member [of] the other nations of the world, a slave or a woman). Since each blessing thanks Hashem for giving a higher level of mitzva observance, one precludes the other, and we should make sure to recite them in order. However, many opinions do not consider the order of these three blessings critical, and permit the complete recitation of all three even if one began with the wrong *bracha* (*Mishna Berura* 46,16).

Socks and Shoes | TUESDAY

Later on we say the two blessings of "Who clothes the naked" and "Who takes care of all of my needs." *Chazal* tell us that the blessing of taking care of our needs refers to shoes. If we already thanked Hashem for clothing, why do we need an additional blessing for shoes?

Walking around barefoot outside is painful and impractical. Shoes allow us to travel from place to place and attend to our daily affairs. Therefore, in addition to thanking Hashem for clothing, we also express gratitude for our shoes, which enable us to function in the world (*Levush*).

Two other morning blessings also refer to clothing. "Who girds us with strength" thanks Hashem for belts, which separate the top and bottom halves of the body. "Who crowns us with glory" thanks Hashem for giving us tefillin and other head coverings. All of these garments have special significance for prayer and modesty, and help us elevate ourselves before speaking to Hashem (*Mishna Berura* 46,9).

Strength to the Weary |

The morning blessings thank Hashem for many of the kindnesses that He bestows on us each day. Most of these blessings are enumerated in the Gemara, and have been recited for thousands of years. However, there is one that is of later origin: "Who gives strength to the weary."

This blessing is not mentioned in the *Talmud*, and was instituted later by the *Geonim*. Although the *Shulchan Aruch* instructs us not to say it with Hashem's Name, the custom has developed to do so along with all of the other morning blessings (*Mishna Berura* 46,22).

Late-night learning, crying babies, last-minute work deadlines and major exams can all lead us to sleep less than our bodies need. Can we recite this blessing if we slept only three hours (or less) and still feel exhausted? We do so even when experiencing sleep deprivation, since Hashem still gives us the strength to carry on. Even if we were up all night long, we can still say, "Who gives strength to the weary" with Hashem's Name.

However, if we did not sleep at all (or less than half an hour), the next blessing, thanking Hashem for "removing sleep from our eyes" (*hama'avir sheina*), is problematic. Similarly, since the *neshama* leaves the body only during sleep, thanking Hashem for "returning our *neshama*" (*Elokai neshama*) would be inaccurate. If a person did not sleep at least half an hour at night, e.g., Shavuos night, he should try to hear these blessings from someone who slept (*Mishna Berura* 46,24).

A Rooster's Crow | THURSDAY

Most blessings are recited *over l'asiasan*, immediately prior to what we are about to do. Saying them immediately before performing an action helps us to internalize the message that is inherent in the act. As the Ritva says, "[Saying a blessing before the act allows us to] first serve Hashem with our *neshama*, and then serve Him with our body" (*Pesachim* 7a).

Some authorities apply this concept to the morning blessings as well. They rule that each one of these blessings should be said right before the action. According to this understanding, when one hears a chicken crow one says, *hanosen l'sechvi bina,* "Who gives understanding to the rooster" (*Rambam* and *Shulchan Aruch* 46,1).

Others rule that the concept of *over l'asiasan* does not apply to these blessings. Since they were established to praise Hashem for the world He created, they can be made even if one does not actually experience what he is expressing (except for the blessing of *hama'avir sheina*). Based on this explanation a person may recite *hanosen l'sechvi bina* even if he does not hear a rooster crowing (*Rosh* and *Rema* 46,1).

Although Ashkenazim follow the second understanding and make these blessings in all situations, the first understanding still affects the way they make them. In order to feel the maximum gratitude to Hashem with each blessing, one can act out what he is mentioning. Before reciting *poke'ach ivrim* (gives sight to the blind), he can close his eyes and open them, and prior to saying *zokef kefufim* (straightens the bent), he can lean over and straighten himself out (*Yesod V'Shoresh Ha'avoda, Sha'ar Ashmoros* Ch. 4).

According to His Will | FRIDAY

Women do not recite, "Who did not make me a man." Rather, they thank Hashem, "Who made me according to His will." Ashkenazim make this blessing with Hashem's Name, while Sephardim do not mention Hashem's Name (*Ben Ish Chai, Vayeshev* 10). What is the deeper meaning of this blessing?

Hashem initially created man and woman as one entity (*Eruvin* 18a). After seeing their difficulty in functioning as one being, He split them and made the woman a separate entity from the man. This way, each of them would be able to carry out their respective functions properly.

Although human beings are incapable of fathoming why Hashem does something and then changes it, one thing is clear. G-d originally created man in a certain way and then modified him. However, after He created woman, He did not alter His creation in the slightest. In this light, women thank the One "Who made me according to His will," for Hashem has remained constant in His will for womankind from the sixth day of creation to the present moment.

For some decades, secular society has been dominated by views that women have to strive to prove their equal status to men, if not their superiority. Nowadays, when Jewish women regularly leave the home and enter a workforce that was once dominated by men, they must be careful not to be ensnared by this way of thinking. Women should be proud that Hashem's will for them was distinct and ordained from the moment of their creation.

We are given a myriad
of presents daily.
Reciting the morning blessings
helps us to appreciate
these gifts.

4

Small Sacrifices

Understanding Parshas Korbanos

Averting War | SHABBOS

The year was 1991, and world attention was focused on Israel, which was under threat of missile attack from Iraq. The government feared that chemical weapons would be used, and everyone lined up to collect their gas masks, as Israel prepared for the worst possible scenario.

Frustrated with the atmosphere of fear that filled the air, one night I called one of the great Rabbanim of America to ask if there was anything special that I could do to prevent an attack. I expected that he would advise me to make some dramatic change in my life, and was surprised by his simple answer.

"Come to shul five minutes early every morning so that you can make sure and say *Korbanos*," he advised, referring to the passages describing the offerings in the Temple that are meant to be recited every morning before services begin.

"Five minutes early!" I responded in amazement. "That's all we need to do to prevent war?"

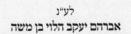

The rabbi responded with equal astonishment, "I told you to get to shul five minutes early to say *Korbanos*, and you say, 'That's all'? Do you have any idea how important it is to say *Korbanos*?"

When the Temple stood, the merit of the offerings brought there protected us from our enemies. Today, as the Temple lies in ruins, reciting *Korbanos* remains our primary line of defense. Let us investigate the halachos of this vital part of the morning services, so that we can ensure that we benefit from the full measure of their protection in these uncertain times (see *Kaf Hachaim* 1,36).

Korban Tamid | SUNDAY

By reciting the Torah's description of the sacrifices, it is considered as if we actually offered them (*Taanis* 27b). Our Sages arranged our recitation of these verses as if we were actually bringing an animal as a sacrifice on the altar. For this reason familiarity with the halachos of these sacrifices is important, for they can help us feel as if we were actually involved in making the offerings in the Temple.

Every morning and afternoon in the *Beis Hamikdash*, the *Korban Tamid* (the daily offering) was brought. Today the Temple is no longer standing, but we can still recreate this service by reciting the eight verses which describe it (*Bamidbar* 28: 1–8). Although most women do not recite *Korbanos* nowadays, it should be noted that some authorities obligate them to recite the verses describing the *Korban Tamid* (*Graz* 47,10), as well as the other *Korbanos* (*Biur Halacha* 47 [end]).

Korbanos were only offered in the Temple by day. Based on this halacha, one should try to recite the *Korbanos* during daylight hours. If a person has to pray early and will not have sufficient time to say *Korbanos* after it gets light, he may recite them before dawn (*Mishna Berura* 1,17). However, special effort should be made to say the *Korban Tamid* by day since the Torah explicitly states that this is the time for this sacrifice (*Makor Chaim* 1,6).

The *Korban Tamid* was a mandatory sacrifice. Therefore, many halachic authorities consider the recitation of *Tamid* verses an obligation. They rule that if a person did not recite it at the beginning of his prayers, he should say it afterwards (*Graz* 48,1; *Orchos Yosher* p. 95).

Standing Up | MONDAY

As mentioned previously, our Sages tell us that reciting the Torah verses of *Korbanos* is like bringing an offering in the Temple. This description raises a fundamental question. Are we like the *yisrael*, the regular Jew who was the owner of the animal, or like the *kohen*, the priest who performed the sacrifice in the Temple?

Some halachic authorities consider the person saying *Korbanos* to be like a *kohen*. In the Temple, *kohanim* were always standing up when they offered *Korbanos*. Since the recitation of *Korbanos* is meant to represent the Temple service, some authorities rule that the passages should be said while standing.

Other authorities argue that the person who says *Korbanos* represents the *yisrael,* who brought the animal to be offered. Therefore, they maintain that one may sit when reciting the verses. Many authorities state that while the verses of the *Korban Tamid* should be said standing up, the other verses may be said while seated (*Mishna Berura* 48,1).

The *Aruch Hashulchan* offers a fascinating compromise between these opinions, bringing the Temple service to life in our times. He rules that a *kohen* should recite the *Korbanos* standing, similar to the way he performed the offerings in the Temple. *Levi'im* and *Yisraelim* can say this section sitting down, since they did not participate in the actual sacrifice in the Temple (*Aruch Hashulchan* 1,26).

Incense Offerings | TUESDAY

While many of the sacrifices served as atonement for our transgressions, the *ketores* (incense offering) had a different goal. Its purpose was simply to bring joy to Hashem, as the verse testifies: "Oil and incense gladden the heart" (*Mishlei* 27).

While in a state of joy, Hashem removes any traces of harsh judgment from the world (*Medrash Tanchuma, Tetzaveh* 15).

The *Zohar* adds: "If a person feels that bad things are happening in his life and nothing that he does is successful, he should meticulously recite the section of the *ketores* every morning and afternoon. If he does this, as well as repenting to Hashem, his situation will improve drastically" (*Vayakel* 219a). Saying this section is auspicious for financial prosperity, especially when written on parchment by a *sofer* (*Seder Hayom* p. 53).

The *ketores* contained eleven ingredients, and a *kohen* who offered incense which lacked even one of them was subject to the death penalty. The Rema suggests that a person who skips a word of the verses describing the incense offering may be liable for a similar punishment. Based on this, some Jews in the Diaspora have the custom to only recite these verses on Shabbos and Yom Tov, when their schedules are more relaxed, so they can make sure that they recite these words carefully (*Rema* 132,2).

Others argue that the death penalty applies only to a *kohen* in the Temple, and not to someone in our age who merely left out a word while reciting the *ketores* verses. Even a *kohen* who offered incense that was missing an ingredient would be punished only if it was intentional (*Beis Yosef*). However, while taking time constraints into account, one should still try to say the *ketores* section carefully every day (*Mishna Berura* 132,17).

Four individuals are obligated to thank Hashem through a *Korban Todah* (thanksgiving offering). People who recovered from illness; were freed from jail; crossed the sea; or crossed the desert. This sacrifice is marked nowadays in the verses of the *Korbanos* section, in Psalm 100 (*Mizmor l'sodah* - A Psalm of Thanksgiving), which is recited as part of *Pesukei D'zimra*, and in the eighteenth blessing of the *Shemoneh Esrei (Modim)*.

The offering of a *Korban Todah* was a sublimely joyous experience. One way that this *simcha* was expressed was that the *Korban Todah* was accompanied by *nesachim*, a wine libation which was poured onto the altar. Based on this service, some include the verses describing the *nesachim* as part of *Korbanos* (*Mishna Berura* 1,14).

Another expression of this joy is found in the way we recite Psalm 100, *Mizmor l'sodah*. "*Mizmor l'sodah* should be sung with a tune for [when the final redemption comes] all of the [current] songs and praises will no longer be said, with the exception of *Mizmor l'sodah*" (*Shulchan Aruch* 51,9). Even if a person does not sing these words, he should be careful to recite *Mizmor l'sodah* with special joyfulness (*Chaye Adam* 18,1).

A final joyous aspect of the *Korban Todah* was that it consisted of forty loaves of bread, of which thirty-six were eaten as part of a festive meal after the offering of the *Korban*. Since ten of these loaves were *chametz*, and *chametz* is prohibited from the middle of the day before Pesach, the *Korban Todah* was generally not brought on that day. As a result, Ashkenazim do not recite *Mizmor l'sodah* on the morning before and during Pesach and on *erev Yom Kippur* (*Rema* 51,9), though many Sephardim do.

Other *Korbanos* | THURSDAY

The fifth chapter of Mishna Tractate *Zevachim* ("*Eizehu makoman*") describes precisely where in the Temple each of the *Korbanos* was offered. Since most of the different sacrifices are mentioned there, these sections of the Mishna were incorporated into the *Korbanos*.

By saying these words, it is considered to some extent as if one offered that particular sacrifice. On weekdays, some people preface each of the *Korbanos* with the words, "If I am obligated to bring a *Korban* _____, this recitation should be considered as if I brought it." On Shabbos and Yom Tov voluntary sacrifices were not offered, and so this statement is not made (*Mishna Berura* 1,17).

The offering of a *Korban* in the Temple was an involved process that required extensive knowledge and training accompanied by pure and lofty intentions. When the average Jew of today merely reads the words of these passages, it may seem like a paltry substitute for the Temple service. In order to infuse one's recitation closer with a true conception of the *Korbanos*, halachic authorities recommend learning these sections in depth with their commentaries. Studying the *Korbanos* in order to achieve a deeper understanding is considered like actually bringing the sacrifices (*Biur Halacha* 1,5; *Mishna Berura* 48,1).

Troubled Times | FRIDAY

Nowadays, due to pressured morning schedules, many Jews are lax about saying the *Korbanos* section, since it has a lower halachic priority than the prayers that follow it. Nonetheless, in times of crisis in the world, one should make a special effort to say *Korbanos*. This protect us from the conflicts that surround us, and act as a safeguard during these troubled times (*Kaf Hachaim* 1,36).

One of the most powerful parts of *Korbanos* is the verse, "You should slaughter the sacrifice on the *tzaphona* (northern side) of the altar before Hashem" (*Leviticus* 1,11). Hashem has promised that whenever someone recites this verse, Jew or non-Jew alike, He will remember *Akeidas Yitzchak* and bring them salvation (*Vayikra Rabba* 2,10 as cited by the *Shulchan Aruch* 1,8). What connection does this verse have to *Akeidas Yitzchak*, and why are these words so important?

Aside from meaning "north," the Hebrew word "*tzaphona*"

has two other connotations. *"Tzaphon"* implies "hidden," while simultaneously meaning "to see." Both these definitions are connected to *Akeidas Yitzchak*, whose reward is hidden from man and seen only by Hashem. The word *"tzaphon"* in the *Korbanos* recalls the *akeidah* and is a key that opens the gate to Divine Assistance (commentary of *Matnas Kehuna* and *Maharzu* on *medrash*).

This verse is also connected to the verse, "The evil starts from the *tzaphon* (north)" (*Jeremiah* 1,14). This refers to the land of Bavel (currently Iraq), which has been a source of strife for the world in both the past and in the present. Reading this Torah verse, which makes mention of the north, guards us from the evil that lurks in the north (*Baal HaTurim, Vayikra* 1,11).

> *Our Sages promised us that the recitation of Korbanos will protect us from all danger.*

5

Special Signs

Understanding the Symbolism in Pesukei D'zimra

Of Bombs and Bandages | SHABBOS

During the Gulf War, I was single and studying in Israel. It was a difficult time for all those learning in yeshivos, because many concerned parents were calling their children back home to America. Those of us whose parents were gracious enough to let us stay merited seeing Hashem's Providence daily.

At the time, I was also involved with shidduchim, and a number of suggestions had come up. However, due to the war, those whom my rebbes deemed suitable had left the country before we had a chance to meet. In my heart, I knew that it was for the best, because anyone I did not meet was obviously not my intended, but nonetheless it left me with a feeling of loneliness. This was compounded by the fact that I had just become part of the large student population of Yeshivas Mir and did not know a soul there.

לע"נ משה בן חנוך

One morning, I woke up early and called a friend in America, hoping to receive some encouragement. Instead of the pleasant words of consolation that I had expected, I was bombarded with criticism. Our Sages tell us that the tongue has the power of life and death, and I felt devastated as I went to the morning prayers.

Each word was a struggle to get out of my mouth, and in the middle of Pesukei D'zimra I felt that I no longer had the ability to continue. I put my head down and for a few minutes sat there quietly. Finally, I gathered up the emotional energy to continue, and noticed that my finger had remained on the place where I stopped.

To my amazement it was the verse, "He [Hashem] heals the brokenhearted, and bandages their hurts" (Tehillim 147:3). I felt consoled and knew that Hashem would help heal my wounds. A week later, I met my future wife, and soon we were engaged.

During that difficult time, Hashem gave me a special sign that encouraged me and helped me to continue to pray. In fact, Pesukei D'zimra entails a number of practices designed to inspire us all to greater heights of prayer every single day. Let us investigate the halachos of some of these customs.

Rising Up |

Our Sages reveal that 2,000 years ago a piece of paper was seen falling from the heavens. Inscribed on it were the eighty-seven words that constitute the *Baruch She'amar* prayer which the Great Assembly decided should be the opening blessing to *Pesukei D'zimra* (*Mishna Berura* 51,1).

The Arizal writes that when a man recites *Baruch She'amar*, he should hold the two front *tzitzis* of his *tallis* in his right hand. After completing this prayer he should kiss these *tzitzis* (*ibid.*). What can we learn from this custom?

We begin the morning prayers by reciting *Korbanos*, paralleling the sacrificial service in the Temple. *Baruch She'amar* marks the transition into the next section of the prayers. Lifting up *tzitzis* represents lifting ourselves up from the section of *Korbanos* to that of *Pesukei D'zimra* (Rabbi Munk, "*The World of Prayer*"). In fact some have the custom to hold their *tzitzis* from the start of the *V'Yivarech David* passage until the conclusion of *Pesukei D'zimra*, in order to mark the transition to the *Shema* section of the prayers (*Siddur Ish Matzliach*).

On Tisha B'Av, we mourn the destruction of the *Beis Hamikdash* and the discontinuation of the sacrificial service. Although we are obligated to say the *Korbanos* as part of our prayers every morning, at this time we are meant to feel their loss more than on other days. In order to demonstrate our mourning and show that since we no longer have real *Korbanos* we cannot make a proper transition, a man does not lift up his *tzitzis* during *Baruch She'amar* on Tisha B'Av (*Abudaraham*).

An Open Hand | MONDAY

After concluding *Hodu* (or after *Baruch She'amar*, according to *Nusach Sephard* and *Sephardim*), we say Psalm 100, "*Mizmor l'sodah*," thanking Hashem for the numerous hidden and open miracles that He performs for us on a daily basis (see previous "Small Sacrifices" chapter). Afterwards we say *Yehi Chevod*, a compilation of verses which mention Hashem's name eighteen times. We then proceed to *Ashre*i, which marks the beginning of the main section of *Pesukei D'zimra*.

Our Sages promised that anyone who says *Ashrei* three times a day is guaranteed a place in the World to Come. Why is *Ashrei* so important? The Talmud offers two reasons: First, each verse of Psalm 145, the main part of *Ashrei*, starts with a different letter of the Hebrew alphabet. Secondly, *Ashrei* contains the verse "*pose'ach es yadecha*"(You [Hashem] open Your Hand, and sustain the needs of all living creatures)*,* which affirms Hashem as the Source of all sustenance (*Brachos* 4b).

"*Pose'ach es yadecha*," which attributes all worldly sustenance to Hashem, is the most significant verse of *Ashrei*. A person must recite this verse with proper concentration, and should repeat it if he failed to do so (*Shulchan Aruch* 51,7). If one only realizes latter in *Pesukei D'zimra* that he failed to concentrate properly, he should say it again, and then continue with the verses that follow it (*Mishna Berura* 51,16).

These aspects of *Ashrei* make it the most critical section of *Pesukei D'zimra*, so much so that if a person came late to prayers, he may skip all of the *Pesukei D'zimra* in order to recite *Shemoneh Esrei* with a *minyan*, but *Ashrei* (in addition to *Baruch She'amar* and *Yishtabach*, as well as *Nishmas* on Shabbos) must be said first. Because it is so important, halachic sources suggest a number of active gestures to promote concentration at this critical point in prayer.

Symbolic Gestures | TUESDAY

Throughout Jewish history there have been many incidents where an action gave power to words. One of the most dramatic examples involved the prophet Elisha and King Yoash when the Jewish people were at war with Aram. Elisha told King Yoash to shoot an arrow, and then said, "This is the arrow of G-d's deliverance, and the deliverance from Aram; you shall fight Aram at Afeq until you destroy them."

Afterwards, Elisha told King Yoash to take his arrows and smash them on the ground, symbolizing the destruction of Aram, the enemies of the Jewish people. King Yoash pounded them into the ground three times. At the conclusion of the story,

Elisha revealed to the king that had he done this five or six times he would have completely annihilated Aram (*Melachim* II 13: 15-19).

From this incident, we see the power of symbolic gestures. Halachic authorities apply this idea to *Ashrei*, and suggest that while reciting the verse *"Pose'ach es yadecha"* one should turn up one's palms (*Ben Ish Chai, Vayigash* 12; *Makor Chaim* 51,7). Opening our hands shows that we are ready to receive the abundant flow of blessing from Above, and helps us relate to the special power of this verse.

Some men have a custom to touch their tefillin while reciting this verse. Touching one's tefillin while reciting *"Pose'ach es yadecha"* shows the connection between performing mitzvos and the fulfillment of one's material needs. This small gesture reflects the ultimate purpose of Hashem's sustenance of His creations: that we may do His will (*Taamei Haminhagim* p. 549).

The Art of Giving | WEDNESDAY

Our Sages taught us that Hashem generally treats a person the way that he treats his fellow man, measure for measure. Therefore, before approaching Him with prayers to sustain us, it is proper to demonstrate that we, too, are givers. Based on this, some people have the custom to give charity while they are reciting "*Pose'ach es yadecha*" (*Seder Hayom*).

According to the Arizal, a person should give charity during the "*V'Yivarech David*" passage right after the verse "*v'haosher v'hakavod milfanecha*" (and the wealth and honor are before You). While saying the words which follow, "*v'Atah moshel b'kol*" (and You rule over everything), he should give over the money (*Mishna Berura* 51,19). Whichever of these practices is followed, the act of opening our hearts and hands to the poor opens the Heavenly Gates of Mercy and allows our prayers to be heard.

The *Zohar* reveals a deeper level of symbolism in this gesture of charity. The two hands of the people giving and receiving the money each have five fingers, and represent the Hebrew letter *hei*, which has the numerical value of five. When a person's arm is extended to give charity, it looks like the letter *vav*. Meanwhile, the small coin resembles the letter *yud*. These four letters (twice *hei*, a *vav* and a *yud*) come together to spell G-d's ineffable Name of Mercy, symbolizing that by giving charity, we are invoking the essence of Divine Mercy (as cited in the *Kaf Hachaim* 51).

Without Pausing | THURSDAY

"When a person reaches the expressions of praise of Hashem listed in the *Yishtabach* prayer, he should not pause at all. What happens if he interrupts his recitation? A fire comes out from the wings of the angels and says that whoever interrupts the recitation of Hashem's praise should be taken from this world" (*Zohar, Terumah* 132).

The rabbis took the Zohar's dire warning very seriously, and they advise us to be careful to say all of these praises without pause. Although the *Shelah* writes that the fifteen expressions of praise should be said in one breath, the halacha is that it is sufficient to say them without interruption (*Mishna Berura* 53,1).

When a person is a little behind in his prayers, he might find himself still saying *Yishtabach* while the rest of the congregation has moved on to *Kaddish*. Since some authorities consider answering *Kaddish* to be an interruption, one should try and time the praises of *Yishtabach* so that he will not have to answer *amen* in the middle (*Kaf Hachaim* 53,2). If this cannot be avoided, he should answer *amen* and then start the praises again from the beginning (*Ben Ish Chai, Vayigash* 15).

Returning from Battle | FRIDAY

In this chapter we have examined a few of the main practices that help make *Pesukei D'zimra* more meaningful. However, there is one more chance to show our devotion in its conclusion.

"Talking between the conclusion of the blessing of *Yishtabach* and the start of the blessing of *Yotzer* is a transgression, and reason to return from battle in times of war" (*Shulchan Aruch*

54,3). Talking during *Pesukei D'zimra* is forbidden because it creates a break between the opening blessing of *Baruch She'amar* and the closing one of *Yishtabach*. After reciting *Yishtabach* one has already concluded *Pesukei D'zimra*, and one might assume that it would not be so grave to speak then. How can we understand the severity of the *Shulchan Aruch's* warning?

On a simple level, *zimra* means songs, and refers to the *Tehillim* and verses that we say prior to the blessings of *Shema*. However, the word "*zimra*" also alludes to the pruning (of plants), and refers to the cutting away of all of the obstacles that stand in the way of our prayers reaching Hashem. Saying *Pesukei D'zimra* before *Shemoneh Esrei* prunes away these obstructions and allows our prayers to rise to the Heavens unimpeded.

Speaking about mundane matters during or even after *Pesukei D'zimra* rearms these obstructive forces, and empowers them to block our prayers from reaching the Heavenly Throne. If we really want our prayers to be heard, there is only one way: Barring emergency situations, we should not speak of any unrelated matters until the end of the prayers (*Mishna Berura* 54,5).

*The symbolic gestures
performed during Pesukei D'zimra
help us connect to this special
section of prayer.*

6

Kaddish Four

Understanding the Four Types of Kaddish

Life After Death | SHABBOS

Rabbi Akiva once encountered a man with a complexion as black as coal. On his head he was carrying a load too heavy for ten people to bear, and he was running as swiftly as a horse. Rabbi Akiva asked him to stop and explain what he was doing.

"During my lifetime I was a tax collector," the man answered. "I would give the poor a very hard time and be exacting to demand every penny due, yet I did not pressure the rich. After I left this world, the Heavenly Court ordered that as a punishment for my actions, I would have to come back to this world to gather wood to make a fire, in which I am burned up anew every day."

Concerned for this man's unending suffering, Rabbi Akiva asked, "Is there any way you can get out of this situation?" The man replied that if his son could serve as the prayer leader and say *kaddish* and the congregation would answer, *"Amen, yehei shmei rabba,"* he could be saved.

In memory of
Malka bas Dovid and Yehudah ben Aron
from Beth and Steve Baker and Jonathan and Ronni Arden

Rabbi Akiva set out to search for the man's son, but the person he found was so distant from mitzva observance that he did not even have a *bris milah*. After guiding him through his bris, Rabbi Akiva taught him the prayers and *kaddish*, and instructed him on how to be a prayer leader. Shortly afterwards, in the merit of his son's *kaddish*, the man was allowed entrance to the next world (*Or Zerua*).

We all recognize the importance of *kaddish*, yet putting our understanding into practice can be difficult. Let us investigate some of the halachos pertaining to this famous prayer, which plays such a central role in the services.

Full *Kaddish* | SUNDAY

There are four types of *kaddish*: full *kaddish*, half *kaddish*, full *kaddish* with an addition (*tiskabel*), and Rabbinic *kaddish*. While all of them share a similar format, each one plays its own distinct role in the flow of the prayers.

Full *kaddish,* like *half kaddish* and *kaddish tiskabel,* is said after prayers which contain verses, such as *Mizmor Shir*, *Aleinu* and *shir shel yom*. This *kaddish* is said by mourners, who, in doing so, provide merit to the soul of their departed relatives (*Rema* 132,2). This prayer is so powerful that even if one's father commands him not to say *kaddish* after he passes on, the child should nonetheless recite it (*Pischei Teshuva* 344,1).

At times there are a number of mourners in shul, all of whom want to recite the *kaddish*. Circumstances permitting, it is preferable for them each to recite *kaddish* individually, since if they recite *kaddish* at the same time, it is difficult to hear each one clearly. If this is not possible, they should make sure to say *kaddish* in unison so that every word can be heard distinctly.

Half *Kaddish* | MONDAY

There are other parts of the services that involve the reciting of verses, but are not followed by a full *kaddish*. For example, there is no full *kaddish* after reciting *Pesukei D'zimra* and after the Torah reading. Why is full *kaddish* not said following these sections?

Half kaddish is recited to show that one section of the service has ended and a new part is starting. In order to make this noticeable we recite half *kaddish* instead of the full one (*Mishbatzos Zehav* 55,1).

On the other hand, *Shemoneh Esrei* does not contain any verses, yet when the *Tachanun* prayer is not said, half *kaddish* is recited afterwards. One explanation for this is that although it is true that there are no verbatim verses in *Shemoneh Esrei*, to neccesiate a *kaddish*, nevertheless many of its blessings are based on the wording of verses and it is appropriate to say *kaddish* afterwards (*Mishbatzos Zehav* 55,1). Others explain that immediately before and after *Shemoneh Esrei*, verses are recited ("*Hashem sifasai tiftach*" and "*Yiheyu l'ratzon*"), and therefore one says *kaddish* after its recitation.

Kaddish Tiskabel | TUESDAY

After the "*uva l'Tzion*" ("A redeemer will come to Zion") prayer, at the end of the daily services, we recite full *kaddish* with the additional "*tiskabel*" section, a special supplication that our *Shemoneh Esrei* prayers should be answered. Why do we wait until after *uva l'Tzion* to make this request? Since *Shemoneh Esrei* is closely connected to the prayers which follow it, it is not considered complete until after they are all said.

Although there is only one difference between *kaddish tiskabel* and full *kaddish*, this additional line plays a critical role in our prayers being accepted. If for some reason someone forgot to say this line, it should be added into a later *kaddish* after *Aleinu* or the *shir shel yom* (Rav Chaim Kanievsky, as cited in *Ishei Yisrael* 26,11). On Tisha B'Av when the Jewish people are in a state of mourning, we express our sorrows by omitting this line, as if to show that Hashem has not accepted our prayers (*Rema* 559,4).

At times, two mourners are present in shul, and one of them has to forgo the opportunity to be the *shatz,* to lead the prayers. In such cases they can make a compromise, and the other one can "take over" before the second *Ashrei*. Although the *kaddish tiskabel*, which follows *uva l'Tzion*, is connected to the previous *Shemoneh Esrei*, the second *shatz* can nonetheless say it in place of the first one (*Mishna Berura* 581,14).

Rabbinic *Kaddish*

From the times of the Talmud, rabbis have customarily made public addresses on Shabbos. Our Sages instituted that *kaddish d'rabbanan* (rabbinic *kaddish*) should be recited after these discourses. The rabbi would usually expound on *agadah*, the stories and non-halachic sections of the Talmud, a subject that was of interest to the general populace (*Rashi Sota* 49a; *Mishna Berura* 54,9).

While everyone loves stories, tackling a complex halachic issue in the Talmud may initially be less enjoyable. Since *kaddish d'rabbanan* should be said with joy, our Sages instituted that it should be said specifically after reading passages of *agadah* (*Birkei Yosef* 55,1).

It is customary to recite *kaddish d'rabbanan* even after a class in halacha. In order to fulfill the above ruling, a short passage of *agadah* from Rav Chananya ben Akashya is recited as soon as the class is completed. Care should be taken to recite this passage with great pleasure and enthusiasm (*Kaf HaChaim* 55,3).

The halacha tells us that just like one must avoid extra *brachos*, similarly one must stay away from too many "kaddishes" (*Mishna Berura* 55,1). At times, when one is in a hurry to leave shul, it seems like *kaddish* is being recited too many times. What constitutes "too many kaddishes," and what is the right amount?

The half *kaddishes* said at the ends of section of the services like *Pesukei D'zimra* or after *Tachanun* are obligatory, and no matter what the situation is, they cannot be skipped. Many have the custom to say full *kaddish* both after reciting *Aleinu* and the *shir shel yom*. These *kaddishes* are primarily for people mourning the loss of a parent, though even after the eleven traditional months of *kaddish* have concluded, one may say one of these *kaddishes* for one's parents.

The *kaddish d'rabbanan* recited after *Korbanos* and at the end of the prayers after *ketores* (for those who have this custom) is less binding. Nonetheless, many great Torah personalities made a point of saying them, and according to the Arizal, reciting these *kaddishim* has a major impact on whether one's prayers will be accepted or not (*Shaar Hakavanes - kaddish*). If there is an orphan present he should recite them; otherwise they should be said by the *shatz* (*Pischei Teshuva, Yoreh De'ah* 376,4).

If all of these *kaddishim* are either obligatory or recommended, what is the halacha's intention when it warns against saying too many *kaddishim*? Even though it is praiseworthy to say *kaddish* after a public *shiur*, one should not gather a *minyan* together and have each person say a few words of Torah just so that one can say *kaddish* afterwards (*Mishna Berura* 55,1). Other authorities suggest that at the end of the prayers, if there is no mourner present, reciting all of the kaddishes constitutes "too many kaddishes."

Annulling Decrees | FRIDAY

We are taught that answering "*Amen, yehei shmei rabba*" ("Amen, His Name should become great") during *kaddish* with all of one's might can annul all harsh heavenly decrees (*Shabbos* 119b). Some take this statement literally and rule that one should use all of his physical energy to answer *kaddish* (*Tosfos*). Others maintain that it refers to one's powers of mental concentration (*Rashi*).

The words of our Sages beg the following question: Since Divine justice is very precise, if there is a decree then the person requires this punishment in order to make amends for a transgression. How can he have the decree annulled merely by saying "*Amen, yehei shmei rabba*"?

The purpose of all Divine punishment is to cause us to reflect on our actions so that we redirect ourselves towards serving Hashem properly. When a person says, "*Amen yehei shmei rabba"* with all his strength, holding nothing back, he lifts himself to the height of his powers to sanctify Hashem's Name. Since he has already reached the highest pinnacle of Divine service, there is no longer a need for a harsh decree to motivate him further.

While this might sound easy in theory, in practice this is extremely difficult. Focusing all of one's energy and concentration for every *kaddish* is no simple task, and one could easily miss the mark. At the same time, a person must be careful not to go overboard, since this could cause others to make fun of his actions, which would be a transgression (*Mishna Berura* 55,5 citing *Rabbeinu Yona, Brachos* 13b). Focus and insight are crucial to achieving the right balance, so that one can properly sanctify Hashem's Name.

Answering kaddish raises us
to great heights, and in doing so
we have the ability to erase
all harsh decrees.

7

Foreign Beliefs

Understanding the First Blessing of Shema

Like many young Jews who grew up estranged from their heritage, Suzanne felt a painful void in her innermost core that nothing could fill. She had spent a number of years completing a doctorate in astrophysics; her thesis focused on the origins of the universe, especially the Big Bang theory. With her doctorate completed, she set out to find true meaning in her life.

Her friends advised her to go to India and seek truth there. While traveling in the Indian countryside she encountered members of a strange and ancient religion – Zoroastrianism. She was fascinated to learn their theological view that a "good god" is engaged in an ongoing struggle with an "evil god." While she thought these ideas were intriguing, she did not feel that they satisfied her burning questions, so she continued on her quest.

Soon after, she encountered some church missionaries who

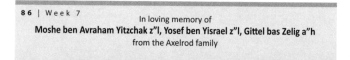
In loving memory of
Moshe ben Avraham Yitzchak z"l, Yosef ben Yisrael z"l, Gittel bas Zelig a"h
from the Axelrod family

were working in rural India. They were more than happy to share their religious philosophy with her. Suzanne listened politely, but she did not feel attracted to the idea of praying to a savior who had died 2,000 years ago.

Finally, Suzanne traveled to a remote mountaintop where she found what she thought she was looking for: a guru who promised to unlock the mysteries of the universe and help her reach ultimate spiritual enlightenment. But after several weeks of trying to meditate and clear her mind of all worldly cares, Suzanne found that she felt more lonely and confused than ever.

When she went to bid the guru farewell, he asked her: "Which religion were you born into?"

"I am Jewish by birth," replied Suzanne.

"If you are searching for truth you should investigate your own religion in Israel," said the guru. "The Jews have truth; they believe that G-d is One. If you go there I think you will find answers to many of your questions."

Figuring she had nothing to lose, Suzanne packed her bags and traveled to Israel. In Jerusalem she attended some classes and spoke to some rabbis. After just a few weeks in seminary, she realized that she had found everything she was looking for and more. This was the life that she had been born to lead.

Suzanne's quest is typical of many *ba'alei teshuva* whose yearning to get close to Hashem leads them to investigate other religions before finally bringing them back to their own religion. But all of us get a taste of such a journey when reciting the blessing that precedes the *Shema* in the morning prayers. Before accepting Hashem's Absolute Oneness and Sovereignty, during *Shema*, we first declare the falsehood of all other beliefs.

Universal Truths | SUNDAY

The scientific theories developed over the past century have focused on explaining the phenomena that make up our universe without reference to G-d. Stars and planets are viewed as inanimate objects that evolved as a result of the Big Bang. The sun's rising and setting and the appearance of the constellations are viewed merely as highly complex astronomical patterns that evolved by chance.

Yet the Rambam writes: "All of the stars and planets are animate entities that have understanding and intellect. They are alive and fully recognize the One Who created the world. Each one praises and glorifies G-d according to its level and its recognition of His greatness" (*Yesodei HaTorah* 3,9).

The first blessing before *Shema* affirms this fundamental tenet: "The Beneficent One fashioned honor for His Name, emplaced luminaries all around His power. The heavenly hosts, holy ones, exalt the Almighty, constantly relating the honor of G-d and His sanctity."

Before accepting Hashem as the only power in the universe, we declare our belief that every aspect of creation willfully serves Hashem.

Darkness by Day | MONDAY

Some religions believe that there are two gods, one of good and one of bad. Whenever something which they consider positive takes place, they attribute it to the god of good, and when something they deem negative happens they say it was from the god of evil. They think that the constant ups and downs of life are a result of the struggles between these two gods.

Judaism views this matter totally differently. We believe that there is one G-d and that everything that takes place in this world comes directly from Him and is good. This belief is reaffirmed twice daily when we say *Shema* and proclaim that Hashem is in fact "*echad*" — The One and Only.

This concept is alluded to in the first blessing preceding the *Shema*. The Talmud tells us that in the opening blessing of *Shema* we must mention the night during the day and the day during the night (*Brachos* 11b).

On the surface, darkness seems less good than the light and warmth of daylight, both literally and figuratively. "Dark times" are usually associated with loss, loneliness, confusion and hardship. And yet in the pre-*Shema* blessing we mention darkness during the day when the sun is shining brightly. This affirms our belief that every creation of Hashem and everything that He causes to transpire upon this Earth is ultimately good (*Rabbeinu Yona, Brachos* 5b).

Taking this idea one step further, we may suggest that the black of the night is in fact something extremely positive. While daylight helps us engage in all the activities we need and is essential for every chemical and biological process on the planet, nighttime signals that it is time to stop and rest and gather strength for the coming day. Symbolically, dark times in our lives are often opportunities to stop and take stock of who we really are and where we really want to go in the future. Mentioning the night by day helps us focus on the positive aspects of the night (*Mahari Abuhav* according to *Perisha* 59,1 and *Elia Rabba*).

Significant Pauses | TUESDAY

Some religions teach that the way to come close to G-d is through an intermediary. Some of these intermediaries are alive, while others have passed on, yet their followers still consider them a conduit to G-d. During the first blessing which precedes the *Shema* we declare our opposition to these erroneous belief systems in a very subtle way.

Halachic authorities note a number of points in the prayer

services where if two consecutive words are uttered in a hasty, slurred manner, a different word with an incorrect meaning could be formed. In order to prevent this, there are a number of points in the service where one should be careful to pause briefly between the words. In some *siddurim*, these places are marked with a slash or dash.

When we come to the word "*mamlichim*" ("declare the kingship of...") in the first blessing before the *Shema*, we do more than pause momentarily. Even though this word is in the middle of a sentence, we stop completely after it and wait for the prayer leader to say·this word out loud. Only then do we continue with the following word – "*es.*"

To understand this practice, it should be noted that if these two words are read quickly they sound like *mamlichim mes* — "declare the kingship of a dead person." In order to show that such a belief is a complete anathema to the Jewish religion, the prayer leader and the congregation make a special point of stopping between these two words (*Chasam Sofer, Shulchan Aruch* 59).

A few lines later, when we arrive at *Kedusha*, we again pause and wait for the *shaliach tzibbur*. The reason for these pauses differs from the earlier one. Since *Kedusha* consists of biblical verses, we do not want to merely repeat them by rote after the *shaliach tzibbur*. We stop to make sure we will read them from the *siddur* (*Magen Avraham*).

Some religions believe that holiness cannot be found in this world, which is mired in physicality, and as such cannot be a source of spiritual enlightenment. They believe in secluding themselves from the mundane distractions of this world, such as family relationships, work and business, and communal affairs. They idealize silent solitude and meditation as the only way one can come close to the Divine.

Judaism takes a radically different approach. We believe that the highest levels of spirituality can be achieved only by engaging in worldly matters. To affirm this tenet of our faith, a number of times during the prayers we repeat the verse, "Holy, Holy, Holy is Hashem, the whole world is filled with His glory."

According to the vision of the Prophet Yeshaya, this statement is proclaimed by the Heavenly Host in praise of Hashem. By calling out this verse in unison, the congregation declares that although G-d's holiness is far beyond anything we can comprehend, nonetheless it surrounds us even in this lowly world, and we can access it here through worldly matters. Like the angels and other celestial beings that Hashem Himself created, we recognize His complete authority over the universe (*Abudaraham*).

Our Sages tell us that the celestial servants of Hashem do not praise Him until we have done so in our prayers. For this reason, some halachic authorities rule that we should not say *Kedusha* ahead of the rest of the congregation (*Makor Chaim* 59,4). However, if one knows that the congregation will rush through that section of the prayers, one may say it slowly beforehand by himself (Rav Chaim Kanievsky as cited in *Ishei Yisrael* 17,27).

Kedusha With a Minyan | THURSDAY

The Rambam writes, "When saying the first blessing of *Shema* without a *minyan*, *Kedusha* should be skipped." However, the Rambam's son later testified that his father retracted his ruling and agreed that *Kedusha* during the blessing before *Shema* may be said even when praying alone (*Teshuvos of the Rambam* 213). Which opinion should we follow in practice?

The *Shulchan Aruch* cites both opinions of the Rambam, reconciling them by ruling that an individual should read *Kedusha* with a melodious tune, as though he were reading from the Torah. When reading *Kedusha* with such a tune, all opinions agree that a *minyan* is not required. Many authorities side with this ruling and advise reading *Kedusha* tunefully, as if one was reading the Torah (*Mishna Berura* 59,12).

Even according to the opinions that a *minyan* is required to respond to the *Kedusha* before *Shema*, it is not necessary for everyone to recite *Kedusha* together. According to all opinions, as long as there are nine other men present, an individual may say *Kedusha* in his own time (*Mishna Berura* 59,11).

In this chapter we have examined how the first blessing of the *Shema* serves to repudiate some beliefs which are foreign to the Jewish religion. However, there is another goal that all the blessings of *Shema* share.

"Seven times a day I praise You because of Your righteous statutes" (*Tehillim* 119,164). Based on this verse, the Great Assembly determined that seven blessings should be recited before and after the morning and evening *Krias Shema* (*Brachos* 11a). But why did they understand this verse to refer to blessings surrounding the *Shema*?

Throughout history, many Jews have been put to death for being Jewish. As is well-known, these martyrs always uttered the words of the *Shema* with their last breath. The *Shema* proclaims the fundamental Jewish tenets: that G-d's Oneness is indisputable, that everything He does is absolutely good, and that all of His statutes are righteous. While at times this may be difficult for us to understand, due to our limited perception of reality, the absolute truth of this statement is deeply embedded in the heart of every Jew.

When faced with enemies who will stop at nothing to destroy the Jewish people, Jews have always found the strength to face their fate *al kiddush Hashem* – to die proclaiming Hashem's Oneness. However, the Great Assembly understood that the willingness to die by the *Shema* is not enough. We have to *live* by the *Shema*; we need to face each day with an awareness of Hashem's Oneness. They instituted the requirement that we praise and thank Hashem for the privilege of saying *Shema* when our lives are *not* at stake.

These seven blessings before and after the *Shema* give us a daily opportunity to express our joy in proclaiming the Oneness of Hashem. Just as a bride and groom express the joy of their union with seven blessings under the wedding canopy; so too, we express our joy in acknowledging Hashem's Oneness through the Shema by saying seven blessings before and after its recitation each day.

Before accepting Hashem's Absolute Oneness and Sovereignty, during Shema, we first declare the falsehood of all other beliefs.

8

Eternal Love

Understanding the Second Blessing of Shema

Tears for Torah | SHABBOS

Rav Naftali Tzvi Yehuda Berlin — known as the Netziv — was renowned for his tremendous diligence in Torah learning. At a young age, he took upon himself to learn twelve hours a day every single day of the year. Day in and day out, he was always studying Torah with passion and fervor.

One year, shortly after the Yom Kippur services had concluded, his father–in–law and a few other Torah scholars were walking home. They heard the sweet sounds of Torah learning and went to see who could be studying so soon after the fast's conclusion. The Netziv's father-in-law smiled when they peered into the room and saw the Netziv already deeply engrossed in his learning.

Although the Netziv literally invested his whole life in his studies, he still attributed his success in becoming one of the greatest Torah scholars and leaders of his generation to his

Dedicated in honor of
Emuna Malka and Temima Esther Feinberg
by their parents, Lauren and Daniel Feinberg

prayers. With the exception of Rosh Hashana, when some say that crying is forbidden, his tears would flow freely every day, twice a day, when he said the blessing of "*Ahava Rabba*" ("abundant love") before *Shema*. He testified that on a day when he did not cry during this prayer, he did not have insights in his Torah learning (heard from Rav Shlomo Brevda).

The story is told of a student who visited Volozhin, where the Netziv was Rosh Yeshiva. Towards evening, the visitor prepared to leave but his host urged him to stay until the next day for the morning services. He told him that just seeing the way that the Netziv recited the prayer of *Ahava Rabba* would change his entire life (heard from Rav Don Segal).

Why is it that the Netziv and other Torah giants placed such emphasis on *Ahava Rabba*, and attributed their success in life to reciting this prayer with intense emotion? The answer clearly lies beyond its movingly poetic composition. Rather, Hashem's deep love for the Jewish people is expressed in this blessing a number of times. By examining these expressions we come to a deeper understanding of Hashem's great love for us and form a deeper, more passionate relationship with Him and His Torah.

Abundant Love | SUNDAY

"One should not start the second blessing of *Shema* with the words 'eternal love' (*ahavas olam*); rather, the blessing should open with the words 'abundant love' (*ahava rabba*). Others say that the correct way to start the blessing is with the words 'eternal love,' as the verse says [*Yirmiyah* 36], 'With an eternal love I [Hashem] love you'" (*Brachos* 11b).

What is the difference between the abundant and eternal love discussed in the above Talmudic passage? And why do some authorities rule one should be said in the morning and the other in the evening?

Ahava rabba, abundant love, refers to the immense love that Hashem has for the Jewish people, which in practical terms can be seen most clearly in the daylight hours through the untold blessings and wonders He has bestowed on our world and our lives. *Ahavas olam*, eternal love, reminds us that Hashem's love of Israel is everlasting and unwavering. It is mentioned in the evening prayer, since in the "dark times" Hashem's love may not be so clearly perceptible (*Maharal, Nesiv Ha'avoda*, Ch. 7). Based on this interpretation, Ashkenazim say "abundant love" in the morning and "eternal love" in the evening (*Tosfos ibid.*; *Rema* 60,1).

Sephardim, on the other hand, follow the second opinion expressed in the Talmud, and always start the second blessing before *Shema* with the words "eternal love" (*Shulchan Aruch*

60,1). The Arizal also followed this custom, and the *siddurim* of *Nusach Sephard* begin this blessing with the words "eternal love" (as cited in *Shaarei Teshuva* 60,1).

Precious Gifts | MONDAY

Hashem's abundant and eternal love was conveyed to the Jewish people in a grand manner when He gave us His Torah. We, in turn, express our reciprocal love for the Torah in the various passages of the blessing of *Ahava Rabba*. We pray that we will share in the learning of scholars, that we will have deep Torah insight and that our children will follow in its ways.

As part of this *bracha* we say the words, *"l'kayeim es kol divrei talmud Torasecha,"* to uphold all the words of Your Torah. Our Sages tell us that *kiyum* – support – of Torah refers to financial support of Torah scholars. Anyone who contributes to support Torah scholars will receive reward in the next world as a partner in their Torah study.

What should our intentions be when we ask Hashem, *"v'ha'eir eineinu b'Torasecha,"* – to illuminate our eyes with Your Torah? Some say that this request is for insight into the Zohar and the other mystical parts of the Torah (Responsa *Ruach Chaim* as cited by *Kaf HaChaim* 60,3). Others explain that the prayer asks that one's children should be involved with Torah learning (*Ateres Zahav* 47).

"V'lo neivosh l'olam va'ed" - we should never, ever be ashamed. When saying these words we should think about our children and grandchildren. If we instill within them Torah values while they are young, then they will be a source of pride to us in this world and in the next, and we will never be ashamed of them (*Kaf HaChaim, ibid.*).

Never Forget | TUESDAY

While we should try to retain all the Torah we learn, there are certain sections that we are obligated to keep in mind daily. In fact, there are six events in our history that the Torah instructs us to remember constantly. Some halachic authorities extrapolate that this obligates us to mention the verses referring to these events every day. Many *siddurim* list these *"zechiros"* (remembrances) at the end of the morning services.

The Arizal writes that these remembrances are a Torah obligation, which is fulfilled by reciting the *Shema* and its related blessings. The first remembrance – the Exodus from Egypt – is mentioned explicitly at the end of the *Shema*, where the rememberance of Shabbos is also hinted to. The Arizal reveals that the remaining four *zechiros* are alluded to at the end of the second blessing before the *Shema*.

The Jews are known as the Chosen Nation, and the way that we were chosen was by accepting the Torah. While standing at

Mount Sinai, we reached the highest level of closeness that a human being can possibly achieve with his Creator. When we say the words *"uvanu vacharta"* – "You chose us" - we should remember that we were chosen by Hashem to receive the Torah and *"v'keiravtanu"* – "You drew us close" - we should keep in mind the powerful experience of Mount Sinai.

After accepting and receiving the Torah, the Jewish people were catapulted to the highest spiritual level, and our mere existence sanctified Hashem's Name. At that very time, Amalek attacked us in order to decrease the awe of Hashem's Name in the world. Amalek's attack is the third of the daily remembrances. When we say *"l'shimcha hagadol"* – "Your great Name" - we should keep in mind how Hashem's honor was lowered by Amalek's attack following the giving of the Torah.

Following this incident with Amalek, the Jews traveled in the desert for forty years. During this time, Miriam made a slightly disparaging remark about her brother, Moshe Rabbeinu. Miriam's mistake and her punishment are the fifth of the daily remembrances. When we say *"l'hodos"* – "to give thanks" - we should remember that the tongue was created to praise Hashem and not to ensnare us in forbidden speech (as cited in *Magen Avraham* 60,2).

No Beginning | WEDNESDAY

We must keep in mind that when we pray, we are conversing with Hashem. The first thing we say should be an expression of both praise and humility before Him. Therefore, *brachos* generally start with the word "*baruch*," which has the dual implication of both increasing Hashem's honor and bending our knees before Him.

However, two of the *brachos* of *Shema*, *Ahava Rabba* and *Emes V'Yatziv*, do not start with the word "*baruch*." Why is this so?

These blessings are considered "*brachos samuchos*," blessings which are joined to other ones. Since they are preceded by *brachos* that start with "*Baruch Atah Hashem*," they are considered to share in the *baruch* of these blessings. Even though *Emes V'Yatziv* is separated from a *baruch* by the words of *Shema* which precede it, this is not considered an interruption since it is all following the same theme (*Mishna Berura* 54,1).

Not *Birchas Shema* | THURSDAY

Although the blessings before the *Shema* are called "*Birchos Krias Shema*," they do not actually make any reference to the *Shema*. Most halachic authorities explain that these *brachos* are not blessings on *Shema*. This has an important ramification regarding the latest time when the *brachos* may be said.

The Torah writes that *Krias Shema* should be said when a person gets up in the morning and before he goes to sleep. Kings are generally the last to arise in the morning, and even they get up by the first quarter of the day. Consequently, *Shema* must be recited before the end of the first quarter of the day, i.e., within three halachic hours.

The *brachos* before *Krias Shema* are not connected to the time when kings wake up, and they have different halachos. They may be said until the end of the first third of the day, i.e., four halachic hours (*Shulchan Aruch* 58,6). Therefore, even if one misses the time of *Shema*, he can still say the *brachos* in the appropriate time before the end of the first third of the day.

What should a person do if, due to extenuating circumstances, he will only be able to say *Shema* with *brachos* after the first third of the day? In such a scenario a person should say Shema without *brachos* before the first quarter of the day, and make sure that he recites the *brachos* before the end of the first third of the day. Even though the recitation of the *brachos* will be after the allotted time for saying *Shema*, he should read *Shema* again together with the *brachos* (*Shulchan Aruch* 60,2).

Just as the *brachos* are not directly related to the *Shema*, neither are they connected to each other. Even if one mistakenly mixes up the order, he still fulfills his obligation. (*Mishna Berura* 60,5).

The Power of Light | FRIDAY

When creating the world, G-d created two types of light. The first was the radiance of the sun and moon, from which we benefit during the day and night. This light, which allows our eyes to see so that we can physically function in this world, is mentioned during the first blessing of the *Shema*.

In addition to the physical light, our Sages tell us that Hashem also created a spiritual illumination that allows us to perceive the deeper meaning of Creation and our existence. In order to prevent the forces of evil from misusing this second form of light, Hashem hid it within the Torah. Thus, He assured that only those who study Torah with effort and sincerity can benefit from this spiritual form of light.

Every human being appreciates the physical light of the sun by day and the moon by night. However, if we were to try to understand the world by this physical light alone, it would be impossible to comprehend any order or meaning in our existence. Life would seem to be a series of coincidences, some bad and some good, and none of it would make any sense. The physical light of the sun and moon do not help us comprehend the inherent contradictions of life on Earth.

Only the second type of light, the spiritual light of the Torah, gives us the power to understand the deeper meaning of existence. By the light of Torah we can perceive order in the apparent chaos, and good in the seemingly bad. Guided by scholars who have plumbed the depths of the Torah with hard work and sincerity, our lives become full of significance and illumination. The light of Torah, which is described in the second blessing before *Shema*, has the power to transport us to a new plane of existence, completely different from that of the rest of humanity.

The two different types of light described in the two blessings before *Shema* help us recite the *Shema*. If it were always dark, we would not be able to appreciate the beautiful world that G-d fashioned. The first type of physical light described in the first blessing of *Shema* enables us to see the world and accept Hashem as ruler of all Creation.

However, were it only for this first light, we would not be able to say *Shema*. The light of the sun and moon alone may only serve to highlight the contradictions of life and make our acceptance of G-d's absolute dominion through the recitation of *Shema* more difficult. The spiritual light of the Torah mentioned in the second blessing raises us above these questions and gives us the faith and inner strength to wholeheartedly declare *Shema Yisrael.* We thereby accept G-d's sovereignty over the universe even in the darkest times.

*The revelation of the light
of the Torah is one of Hashem's
greatest expressions of His abundant
and eternal love for us.
May Hashem illuminate
our days and nights with the radiance
concealed in the Torah.*

Health Benefits

Understanding Krias Shema

Partners With Hashem | SHABBOS

Once there were two farmers living in Israel. Reuven owned a vineyard in the north and lived in the south, while Shimon owned a vineyard in the south and lived in the north. Each one traveled a great distance to get to work.

One day, Reuven and Shimon met up and realized that there was no reason to travel so far to take care of their respective vineyards. Reuven could tend Shimon's vineyard in the south, and Shimon could tend Reuven's vineyard in the north. This way all of the grapes would be taken care of without the tremendous effort of cross-country commutes (*Midrash Tanchuma, Kedoshim* 6, as cited by *Mishna Berura* 61,6).

Our Sages use this story as a parable to explain the health benefits of reciting *Krias Shema* twice a day. Hashem tells us, "If you accept the yoke of mitzvos anew twice a day by saying *Shema*, I will protect your health." Though the connection between this promise and the above parable is not immediately

In loving memory of our beloved father and teacher
who loved the Torah and Torah Scholars
Elyahu Ambalu HaCohen, Z"L
8th of Adar 5756 – from Aaron C. Ambalu

1 0 7

clear, by delving a little deeper we will come to a profound understanding.

The average person takes some steps to safeguard his health by visiting the local doctor, watching his diet, or exercising regularly. While this is obviously an acceptable, and sometimes essential, way to make sure one will live a long and healthy life, there is a "wonder drug" that obviates the need for putting a great deal of time into the pursuit of health.

Even the greatest doctors have only a partial understanding of how the human body works; none can guarantee a complete cure from an illness. Hashem, on the other hand, has total control of all our bodily processes, and He can certainly ensure good health. For Hashem, healing our bodies is as easy as caring for a nearby vineyard.

Mitzvos, on the other hand, are done in this physical world, and only a Jew, who is a synthesis of the physical and spiritual, can perform them. They are our most valuable spiritual assets, and thus are represented by the second vineyard in our parable. If we undertake to tend the nearby vineyard of mitzvos in this world, Hashem promises us that he will take care of our health, which is difficult for us but easy for Him.

This agreement to tend to our local vineyard, our Sages reveal, is affirmed when we say *Shema* twice a day and accept upon ourselves the observance of the mitzvos. If we do this properly, we can rest assured that Hashem will keep His part of the deal and watch over our health. Let us try to understand the guidelines of how to say *Shema* in a way that will provide us with the maximum health benefits.

248 Limbs | SUNDAY

"There are 248 limbs in the body, and each word of *Shema* serves to protect one of them" (*Zohar Chadash, Rus* 97b). However, when making a tally of all of the sections of *Shema*, one comes up with only 245 words. How do we make up for the three missing words?

"In order to make up the missing three words, the prayer leader should repeat the last three words of *Shema*, *Hashem Elokeichem Emes* (Hashem your G-d is Truth)" (*Shulchan Aruch* 61,3). This is based on the halachic principle of "*shome'a k'oneh*," that when one listens to words it is as if one said them personally. Therefore, these three words, in addition to the 245 words of *Shema*, bring us to the sum total of 248 words.

Ashkenazim who say *Shema* without a *minyan* should not repeat these three words, while the custom of Sephardim is to say them. An Ashkenazi should preface the *Shema* with the words "*Eil Melech Ne'eman*" (G-d, Faithful King). These three words bring him to the desired total of 248.

As stated previously, the *Zohar* reveals that if we are meticulous in reciting the 248 words of *Shema*, Hashem promises to safeguard the 248 limbs of our bodies. While this works well for a man, our Sages tell us that a woman has 252 limbs, four more than a man. How do women make up for these four extra limbs?

Some authorities suggest that although women have 252 limbs, they should follow the same halacha as a man with regards to the extra words of *Shema* (*Responsa Minchas Eliezer* 2,28). This ruling can be understood in light of the *Zohar,* which explains that while a woman's physical body has 252 limbs, her spiritual being only has 248 limbs, parallel to the number of positive mitzvos in the Torah (as cited in *Responsa Revavos Ephraim* 3,200).

Others explain that when a woman recites the entire *Shema*, all of her 252 physical limbs are healed. Healing her 248 spiritual limbs with the words of *Shema* has an effect on her whole body, and as a result her other four physical limbs are taken care of too (as heard from Rav Chaim Kanievsky).

Careful Recitation

"The entire *Shema* should be recited with the same awe as one would feel when reading the proclamation of a king. Every syllable should be said carefully, especially the letters *yud* and *aleph* of the word '*Yisrael*'" (*Shulchan Aruch* 61: 1,18). Why must one be so meticulous about the pronunciation of every letter?

As mentioned earlier, when said properly, every word of *Shema* protects a different limb of the human body. In order for the words to have their full impact, each word must be said correctly. Even a single letter mispronounced could detract from the healing power of the *Shema* (*Mishna Berura* 61,32).

Our Sages reveal that extra care in saying *Shema* cools off the heat of the *Gehenom* that a person endures after death (*Brachos* 15b). Heating oneself up to say *Shema* carefully effectively lowers the heat of *Gehenom* (*Mahari Abuhav* cited by *Beis Yosef* 62,2).

Slurring

In order for *Shema* to have its full impact, exactly 248 separate words must be said. In addition to saying every letter correctly, one should enunciate each word distinctly, without slurring them together. Joining words together detracts from the total and also gives a different meaning to the words.

For example, if the words "*vechara af*" ("anger flared") are said quickly, they sound like "*v'charaf*" ("cursed"). Nobody wants to be the instigator of causing Hashem to curse us, as such a reading implies. Especially in cases where the last letter of one word is the same as the first letter of the next, or the letter *aleph* follows a *mem*, one must take extra precautions to ensure that the two words are not slurred into one (*Shulchan Aruch* 61: 19-21).

The correct pronunciation and clear distinction of each word are crucial for our recitation of *Shema* to have its full impact. Notwithstanding the extreme importance of a careful, slow recitation of the *Shema*, if a person recites the *Shema* quickly, he still fulfills the mitzva of *Krias Shema* (*Shulchan Aruch* 62,1).

Long Life | THURSDAY

"If someone extends the recitation of the word '*echad*' (one) while saying *Shema*, Hashem will extend his days and years" (*Brachos* 13b). Our Sages reveal that aside from protecting each individual limb, the recitation of *Shema* also extends one's life. Why is the word "*echad*" so important?

The most crucial part of the mitzva of *Shema* is the first line. While saying it, a person must keep in mind that Hashem is the only power in the world, and that He is "*echad*," One and Unified in His existence. Without this in mind, a person does not fulfill the mitzva of *Krias Shema* and must repeat it (*Shulchan Aruch* 60,5).

When the letter *ches*, the second letter of *echad*, is inscribed in a Torah scroll it has two humps which form its "roof." This distinctive formation, which alludes to the heavens, symbolizes Hashem's absolute sovereignty over all of the Creation (*Elia Rabba*). In order to instill this within our hearts, the halachic authorities rule that the letter *ches* of the word "*echad*" should be extended slightly to give us enough time to contemplate Hashem's kingship.

The numerical value of the letter *daleth*, the last letter of *echad*, is four. This symbolizes Hashem's rule, which extends to the four corners of the world. The halacha says that a person should extend the letter *daleth* slightly to give himself enough time to contemplate Hashem's dominion throughout the world and beyond. However, practically this is difficult for Ashkenazim to do, and one should be careful not to mispronounce the word by doing so (*Shulchan Aruch* 61: 5,6).

Life-Sustaining | FRIDAY

The *Zohar* reveals how healing results from saying *Shema* meticulously. Every word attaches itself to its corresponding bodily limb and protects it during that day (*Zohar Chadash, Rus ibid.*).

How does this work? Shlomo Hamelech tells us: "The Torah is a tree of life for those who grasp it" (*Mishlei* 3: 18). Torah is life-sustaining and when *Shema*, which is made up of essential words of the Torah, is said properly, each word attaches itself to one limb, protecting it from all harm (*Zohar, ibid.*).

In recent years, healthy living has become a major topic on the agenda in our society. People spend enormous amounts of money and time on health foods, vitamins, exercise and doctors who practice natural medicine to help their bodies function properly.

While taking care of one's health is a Torah obligation, our Sages tell us that saying *Shema* properly should be an integral part of every Jew's daily health regimen. It costs nothing and facilitates healing for each of the 248 bodily limbs, while also providing extension of life and protection from all harm.

"Reciting Shema properly
is the best way to protect our health.
Best of all, saying Shema comes
with a Manufacturer's Guarantee."

Rising above Nature

*Preparing for Shemoneh Esrei
with the Blessing after Shema*

Sudden Death | SHABBOS

The Sage Rebbi Shimon was once walking towards Jerusalem on his way to the Temple. About halfway to his destination he encountered something that caused him to stop abruptly. In the middle of the road lay the body of a man who appeared to have just passed away.

Rebbi Shimon looked into the eyes, nose and mouth of the dead body to try and determine what had caused his sudden death. He did not see any signs of illness or injury and so concluded that he must have died a supernatural death.

Rebbi Shimon concluded: "I am sure that this man did not recite *Emes V'Yatziv* [the blessing after the morning *Shema*] properly."

On a different occasion one of Rebbi Shimon's students suddenly became very sick. Bad turned to worse, and within twenty-four hours his soul had departed from this world. In his

In memory of
Shmuel Abba ben Tanchum Most
from Jordan Most

final moments the student was heard to say that if he had said the blessing of *Emes V'Yatziv* properly he would not have faced such a sudden death (*Zohar* as cited by *Kaf HaChaim* 61,46).

Our Sages reveal that whoever mentions the miracles of the redemption in the blessing of *Emes V'Yatziv* right before saying *Shemoneh Esrei* at sunrise will be protected from all harm that day (*Brachos* 9b, see *Tosfos*). Let us analyze this blessing in order to understand its unique power.

Miracles of Redemption | SUNDAY

By remembering the overt miracles that Hashem has performed throughout Jewish history, we come to recognize the countless hidden miracles that He does for us daily. For this reason He gave us many mitzvos that remind us of these great miracles. Recognizing hidden miracles brings us to a greater awareness of Hashem's presence in our lives, and enables us to fulfill the goal of creation, which is to thank Him (*Ramban* at the end of *parashas Bo*).

How far does this go? The halacha is that anyone who does not mention the plague of killing the firstborn in Egypt, the Exodus from Egypt, the splitting of the sea, and Hashem's kingship in the world does not fulfill his obligation of reciting these *brachos* (*Shulchan Aruch* 66,10; *Mishna Berura* 66,53). For this reason a person should make special efforts to focus while mentioning these miracles (Rav Shlomo Zalman Auerbach as cited in *Ishei Yisrael* 17,55).

Women generally do not have to perform mitzvos which are time-bound. Since the *Shema* and its blessings must be recited by a certain hour of the day, women are technically not obligated to recite them. However, women have accepted upon themselves to say at least the first paragraph of *Shema*, and because of the importance of mentioning the miracles of the Exodus before *Shemoneh Esrei*, many halachic authorities obligate them to say *Emes V'Yatziv* (*Mishna Berura* 70, 2).

Day and Night | MONDAY

During both the day and night services, the blessings after *Shema* start with the word *"emes"* (true). In the morning we say *Emes V'Yatziv* (true and established), while at night we say *Emes V'Emuna* (true and faithful). What significance do these variations have in connection with their assigned time?

"To speak about His kindness in the morning and His faithfulness at night" (*Tehillim* 92). In the daytime, when the world is filled with light and everything is clear, we can easily perceive Hashem's kindness. For this reason during the morning prayers we say *Emes V'Yatziv*, describing all of the open miracles that G-d did for us during the Exodus from Egypt.

During the night, which represents the dark times in our lives, the good in Hashem's actions is much less apparent. Night is a time of *emuna*, because even when we cannot understand what is taking place, we have trust in G-d that He is leading the world towards the final redemption. For this reason, at night we say *Emes V'Emuna,* a blessing that foretells the miracles of the future, which will be even greater than those we experienced when leaving Egypt (*Rashi* and *Tosfos Brachos* 12a).

Because of the direct connection between each of these blessings and the time of day they are recited, one should be very careful to say each one in its proper time. What if one accidentally mixed them up, and started *Emes V'Emuna* in the morning or *Emes V'Yatziv* in the evening? As long as one has not yet said Hashem's Name at the end of the blessing, he should start again. If one already mentioned Hashem's Name, he should complete the blessing and move on (*Mishna Berura* 66,53).

Entering Prayer | TUESDAY

The blessing after *Shema* leads us into *Shemoneh Esrei.* Mentioning the miracles of the Exodus from Egypt puts us in the proper frame of mind for this highest level of prayer. It reminds us that just as Hashem miraculously redeemed us from Egypt, so too He can answer our prayers and grant us everything that we ask for in the *Shemoneh Esrei.*

While the *Shema* and its blessings are said sitting down, *Shemoneh Esrei* must be said standing. When should a person get up? The words *"Tehillos l'Eil Elyon ..."* (Praises to the Almighty ...) hint to the fact that a person is about to begin *Shemoneh Esrei*, which starts off by praising Hashem. For this reason many have the custom to stand up before saying them (*Maharil* cited by *Elia Rabba* 66,9).

Before speaking to Hashem on Har Sinai, Moshe Rabbeinu passed through three separate barriers: darkness, clouds and fog. During prayer we try to recreate Moshe Rabbeinu's experience as much as possible in order to internalize the reality that we are also speaking directly to Hashem (*Kitzur Shelah*). Therefore, after a person stands up he should take three steps forward as if he were crossing these three thresholds (*Rema* 95,1).

Redemption before Prayer | WEDNESDAY

A person is obligated to start *Shemoneh Esrei* immediately after mentioning the Exodus (*Shulchan Aruch* 111,1). Throughout the blessing of *Emes V'Yatziv* we arouse Hashem's love for us by mentioning some of the miracles that He did for us during our redemption from Egypt. The moment we finish this blessing is the most opportune time to petition Hashem for our needs (*Rashi, ibid.*).

Although we talk about the redemption throughout the blessing of *Emes V'Yatziv*, the mitzva not to interrupt only applies after concluding the final blessing of *Ga'al Yisrael*. As soon as one completes this blessing he should start *Shemoneh Esrei*. Even a silent pause for more than a few seconds is considered a break between the mention of redemption and prayer (*Mishna Berura* 111,2).

According to the *Zohar*, answering *amen* to the blessing of *Ga'al Yisrael* that the prayer leader says is not considered an interruption. While the Rema follows this ruling, the *Shulchan Aruch* considers answering *amen* an interruption (*Rema* 111,1).

In order to resolve this dispute, halachic authorities search for ways to circumvent answering *amen*. Some suggest that the prayer leader should say the final words of the blessing *Ga'al Yisrael* silently (Rav Chaim Kanievsky as cited in *Ishei Yisrael* 17,83), while others recommend that each member of the congregation should recite *Ga'al Yisrael* together with the prayer leader (Rav Shlomo Zalman Auerbach as cited in *Halichos Shlomo* 7,18). Whatever practice one adopts, he should make sure to begin *Shemoneh Esrei* immediately afterwards.

Open My Lips | THURSDAY

After accepting Hashem's dominion when reciting *Shema Yisrael* and mentioning many of the miracles that He performed for us as we left Egypt in the blessing of *Emes V'Yatziv*, we are now prepared for *Shemoneh Esrei*. Due to this heightened sense of awe, we should be afraid to speak lest our words fall short, and so we ask: "*Hashem sifasai tiftach*" – Hashem, open my lips (*Abudaraham*).

Most authorities rule that "*Hashem sifasai tiftach*" is a preface to *Shemoneh Esrei*, but not an actual part of it. Therefore, if one forgot to say it, he does not need to repeat *Shemoneh Esrei* (*Biur Halacha* 111,2). Nonetheless, once a person has said, "*Hashem sifasai tiftach*," he may not even answer *amen* (*Mishna Berura* 66,35).

When the *shaliach tzibbur* repeats *Shemoneh Esrei* he says, "*Hashem sifasai tiftach*" softly. This halacha holds true even if there are members of the congregation who are fulfilling their obligation to recite *Shemoneh Esrei* by listening to him. Since they are not verbalizing the words of *tefilla* and only listening to them, they need not hear this verse (*Biur Halacha, ibid.*).

Eternal Reward | FRIDAY

"Anyone who mentions the miracles of the redemption from Egypt before *Shemoneh Esrei* will merit a place in the World to Come" (*Brachos* 4b). Remembering the miracles that Hashem performed for us enables us to recognize Hashem's attribute of kindness and prepares us to beseech Him with the requests of *Shemoneh Esrei*. But how does it help us earn a place in the World to Come?

In the World to Come there is no eating, drinking or any other form of worldly pleasures. Rather, the righteous simply bask in the glory of Hashem's radiance. It is a pure, spiritual joy, without any trace of physicality.

Miracles are also beyond the limitations of this world. Belief in miracles shows that one knows that he is not limited by the natural boundaries that Hashem established in this world, and that one is constantly connected to a higher plane of existence.

By connecting the miracles of the Exodus from Egypt to the miraculous power of our daily *Shemoneh Esrei* prayer, we activate our connection to the spiritual realm. In doing so, we have placed one foot in the World to Come even while we are in this world.

Mentioning the miracles of the Exodus before Shemoneh Esrei helps us internalize the miraculous nature of a Jew's life.

11

Body Language

Understanding the Silent Communication of Shemoneh Esrei

A Desparate Plea | SHABBOS

Yosef and Aryeh were two brothers studying in the Ponovezh Yeshiva. They shared a very close relationship both inside and outside the *beis medrash* and could always be found together.

When Yosef was diagnosed with a terminal illness, his entire family was distraught, and Aryeh especially could not seem to recover from the shock.

Unfortunately, Yosef's situation deteriorated rapidly and his doctors felt that the end was imminent. While the rest of the family kept vigil at the hospital, Aryeh ran into the *beis medrash*, opened up the ark where the *sefer Torah* was kept, and flung himself on the ground, crying to Hashem to heal his brother.

All of the students learning in the *beis medrash* were moved by Aryeh's distress, and they joined forces to say *Tehillim* for Yosef. The walls of the Ponovezh Yeshiva soon shook from the heartfelt prayers for Yosef's recovery. After being immersed in his prayers for some time, Aryeh calmed down. He got up and

In honor of
Jeffery (Ephriam), Sandra (Rachel), Talia (Penina), Zoe (Chava),
and Ethan (Binyamin) Justin

went to join his family at the hospital.

Much to the shock of Aryeh and the rest of the hospital staff, Yosef's condition started to improve. It took some time, but Yosef eventually recovered completely from his illness. It seemed that Aryeh's desperate appeal, along with the fervent prayers of the students of Ponovezh, had been answered (heard from Rav Shlomo Brevda).

Aryeh's actions were a reflection of his passionate need to pour out his aching heart before Hashem in his time of distress. His simple sincerity aroused the mercy of his fellow students, and ultimately the One Above. In the same way, our physical gestures during *Shemoneh Esrei* have the power to express what is beyond words and deepen our communication with Hashem.

While some aspects of this body language have been set down in halachic literature, we are also invited to spontaneously express our emotions during prayer. Let us try to understand the halachos and customs of these gestures, so we can hope to arouse Heavenly mercy when we need it most.

Bowing | SUNDAY

"When Rabbi Akiva would pray by himself, he would bow down with such vigor that he would start his prayers in one corner of the room and finish in another" (*Brachos* 31a). Physically lowering oneself before Hashem shows humility, and is an integral part of prayer. Although intense displays are not appropriate for most situations, our Sages established that one should bow down during *Shemoneh Esrei*.

"When bowing down, a person should bend his body quickly and pick himself up slowly, in order to show that bowing is not a burden. While bending over he should make sure that he moves every vertebra in his spine" (*Shulchan Aruch* 113: 4,6). Our Sages were very specific about how we should bow down in order to express a very distinct message through this form of body language.

"A person should bow down four times during *Shemoneh Esrei*, twice at the start and twice at the conclusion. ... A *kohen gadol* bows at the start and conclusion of each blessing, and a king bends down at the start of *Shemoneh Esrei* and does not raise himself up until he finishes" (*Brachos* 34a; *Shulchan Aruch* 113,1). The greater the Jew's status, the more bowing he needs to do to humble himself before Hashem.

Swaying | MONDAY

"All of my bones should praise Hashem" (*Tehillim* 35,10). How does one accomplish this? By swaying in a back-and-forth motion during prayer, one recruits every part of his body in an effort to sing Hashem's praises (*Rema* 48,1).

The Zohar explains the deeper significance of this body language, which is uniquely Jewish. "A Jew's soul is like a flickering candle. When his soul is ignited by the Torah he learns, it cannot stay still for even a moment, and this causes one's body to sway back and forth" (*Pinchas* 218b).

In one place, the *Mishna Berura* writes that swaying during *Shemoneh Esrei* is praiseworthy (95,7), while in another place he notes that standing still is preferable (48,5). This reflects the fact that sometimes a person may need to sway in order to intensify the emotional power of his prayers, while at other times standing still may be essential for maintaining concentration. Every Jew should decide how best to offer his prayers before Hashem when he prays.

Each person's body language differs, reflecting his individual nature and essence (*Eshel Avraham* 48,4). For this reason, a person should not try to imitate anyone else's gestures (*Noam Elimelech, parashas Kedoshim*). By the same token, a person should avoid unusual or attention-grabbing motions, for this detracts from the main purpose of prayer, which is silent and personal communication with Hashem (*Mishna Berura* 95,5).

Connected Feet

Prayer elevates us above and beyond the confines of this worldly existence. In fact, during *Shemoneh Esrei* we can achieve a level comparable to *malachim*. How do we express this in our *Shemoneh Esrei*?

"And their feet [of Heavenly Beings] are one straight foot" (*Yechezkel* 1,7). Unlike man, who can constantly reach new spiritual heights through performing mitzvos, *malachim* have a fixed spiritual level. Indeed, our Sages described *malachim* as having only one leg, i.e., they are incapable of movement. Therefore, we recite *Shemoneh Esrei* standing with our feet together, demonstrating our elevated angelic stature as we pray (*Mishna Berura* 95,2).

On Yom Kippur, many men wear a *kittel*, a white robe, a gesture which symbolizes our angelic status on this special day (*Rema* 610,4). Angels are generally portrayed as male, and because of this women do not wear a *kittel* on Yom Kippur (*Mishna Berura* 610,16). This raises a question: Must women keep their feet together during prayer?

Some halachic authorities offer a different explanation for why we must keep our feet together. Locked legs is a symbol of our complete dependence on Divine assistance, since we cannot even move without Hashem's help at all times (*Beis Yosef* citing *Mahari Abuhav*). Because of this and other reasons, the accepted custom is that women also keep their feet together during *Shemoneh Esrei* (*Toras Chaim* 95,2).

A person suffering from physical pains or weakness might have difficulty reciting the entire *Shemoneh Esrei* standing with his feet together. Since this gesture is meant to enhance one's concentration and not undermine it, under such circumstances a person is not required to keep his feet together. Yet he should try to do so as much as possible (*Igros Moshe* 5,38).

Hand Positions | WEDNESDAY

"Before *Shemoneh Esrei*, Rava would put his hands on his chest, one resting on the other, like a slave in front of his master" (*Shabbos* 10a). The halacha upholds this practice and recommends holding one's hands in this position during *Shemoneh Esrei* (*Shulchan Aruch* 95,3). Halachic authorities note that this practice depends on the accepted custom for how one stands before a king, and if the custom changes the halacha will also change (*Mishna Berura* 95,6).

The *Shulchan Aruch* writes that one should place his right hand over his left. The left symbolizes the *yetzer hara*, man's negative inclination, while the right symbolizes the *yetzer hatov*, the positive inclination. Putting one's right hand over the left is a sign that the *yetzer hatov* should overpower the *yetzer hara* (*Beis Yosef* 95,3).

The Zohar takes this symbolism one step further. Right symbolizes Hashem's mercy, while left is a sign of strict justice. Placing one's right hand over the left strengthens Divine mercy over harsh judgment during prayer (*Darchei Moshe* 95,3).

Based on this explanation, the Zohar warns against intertwining the fingers of one's right and left hands at any time. Such a formation mixes an element of strict justice with Divine mercy, and is likely to bringing judgment upon oneself (*Zohar* 24a). Especially during prayer, when we are trying to arouse Hashem's mercy, one should avoid interlocking one's fingers (*Be'er Heitiv* 95,3).

Positioning one's hands and other forms of body language are all meant to enhance one's prayers. If such gestures are interfering with concentration, a person is better off taking a different position, such as putting his hands on the table in front of him or letting them hang by his sides. Everyone should recite *Shemoneh Esrei* in a way that is comfortable for conversing with Hashem, avoiding positions that feel awkward or disrespectful (*Shulchan Aruch* 95,3; *Aruch Hashulchan* 91,7).

A Meeting of Eyes |

When people's eyes meet, a deeper level of communication is achieved. For this reason, one of the most important aspects of body language is where we direct our eyes. When reciting *Kedusha*, it is customary to lift one's head towards the heavens as if one's eyes are connecting with Hashem (*Mishna Berura* 125,5).

Closing one's eyes blocks out the physical world and all of the associated distractions. In fact, our Sages said: "Anyone who does not recite *Shemoneh Esrei* with his eyes closed will not merit seeing the Divine Presence when he leaves this world." For this reason, many prefer reciting *Shemoneh Esrei* with their eyes closed (*Mishna Berura* 95,5).

At times, a person might find it helpful to say *Shemoneh Esrei* while looking into a *siddur*. In such a case, it is perfectly acceptable to pray with open eyes (*Mishna Berura* 95,5). Every individual must decide whether to open or close his eyes based on what he feels will promote optimal communication with Hashem (*Mishna Berura* 93,2).

If one chooses to keep his eyes open, he should be careful not to start looking around. Concentration can be maintained only if one is completely focused on prayer and nothing else in the room. Whether one's eyes are opened or closed, his head should be inclined slightly towards the ground (*Shulchan Aruch* 95,2).

Silent Messages

As with all conversations, body language plays a central role in *Shemoneh Esrei*. All of these movements are outer expressions of one's inner feelings, and allow a more profound level of interaction. Yet there is another level of communication that is even deeper and more discreet.

When Yisro was reunited with Moshe Rabbeinu, he advised him, "See among your nation strong, G-d-fearing people of integrity who are not interested in wealth" (*Shemos* 18,21). The wording of this statement raises a question. In light of the fact that we would expect that Moshe would have to seriously investigate people to find out if they were really of such sterling character, how could he be instructed to just "see" them?

The Zohar explains that there are six parts of a person's body that indicate these characteristics. A person's hair, forehead, face, eyes, lips and palms all contain signs of his spiritual level, if we only knew how to read them. Yisro instructed Moshe to look for these signs, and thereby choose the most upright individuals to lead the Jewish people (*Zohar, Yisro* 78a).

A person's actions leave an indelible spiritual mark on these six parts of the body. When we are standing in prayer, even if we do not utter a word, our body signs will speak for themselves. We should be aware that our deeds speak louder than our words, and how we conduct ourselves while not reciting *Shemoneh*

Esrei has a big influence on the power of our prayers when we come before Hashem.

*Our body language
during Shemoneh Esrei
helps us express
the deepest feelings
of our soul.*

Impossible to Praise

Understanding the First Three Brachos of Shemoneh Esrei

Heaping Praise | SHABBOS

Reuven was reciting *Shemoneh Esrei* out loud. Rebbi Chanina happened to overhear him and noticed that he was adding to the standard wording of the prayer. "Blessed is the G-d Who is great, powerful, awesome, mighty, courageous, feared, strong, brave, absolute and honored ..."

Rebbi Chanina waited until Reuven finished. Afterwards he asked him, "Have you completed saying all of the praises of Hashem?! It is impossible to praise Him sufficiently!"

"If so," questioned Reuven, "why does the *Shemoneh Esrei* refer to Hashem as 'great, powerful and awesome'? If we are permitted to use these adjectives, why can't we use more?"

Rebbi Chanina replied: "Moshe Rabbeinu set the precedent, using these three words when he spoke to Hashem [*Devarim* 10,17]. Had he not used these praises already, it would be audacious for us to apply them to Hashem. The Great Assembly later incorporated this phrase into the wording of *Shemoneh Esrei*."

Reuven thought about what Rebbi Chanina said and responded, "I understand that we are incapable of praising Hashem sufficiently. But is there anything wrong with trying to do what we can?"

Rebbi Chanina responded: "Our praise to Hashem implies deficiency. Let me offer the following analogy. If a king had a million coins of gold, and someone praised him for his silver, wouldn't that be considered a disgrace! G-d's greatness is far beyond the capability of human lips to describe, and we should not do injustice to it by attempting to describe it" (*Brachos* 33b).

The first part of *Shemoneh Esrei* is dedicated to praising Hashem in accordance with the formula established by the Great Assembly. The halacha considers the first of these blessings to be one of the most crucial parts of *Shemoneh Esrei*, and complete concentration is mandatory. Let us try to understand these three blessings.

First Blessing:
Actions Speak Louder Than Words | SUNDAY

"Blessed are You Hashem, our G-d and the G-d of our forefathers, G-d of Abraham, G-d of Isaac and G-d of Jacob; the great, mighty and awesome G-d, the supreme G-d, Who bestows beneficial kindnesses and owns everything, Who remembers the kindnesses of the Patriarchs, and brings a redeemer to their children's children, for His Name's sake with love. O King, Helper, Redeemer and Shield. Blessed are You Hashem, Shield of Abraham."

In truth, Hashem does not need our recognition. We praise Hashem for ourselves, in order to place ourselves in the right frame of mind to converse with Him. Praise helps raise our awareness of Hashem's greatness before we approach Him with our requests.

We are not allowed to overdo Hashem's praises in *Shemoneh Esrei*. Yet three full blessings are dedicated towards the goal of praise. If we are forbidden to exceed the three words used by Moshe Rabbeinu, how can we dedicate three full blessings to praise?

As mentioned previously, we are permitted to describe Hashem as "great, powerful and awesome," since these praises were said by Moshe Rabbeinu. The first three blessings serve as proof of these three attributes. Since we are just citing examples of the three permissible praises, recitation of the blessings is appropriate.

The Protocol of Royalty | MONDAY

One of the Chief Rabbis of England was once granted an audience with Queen Elizabeth. Before their meeting, he had been advised exactly what he was supposed to say at every stage of their conversation. He was told not to deviate from this, for speaking improperly to the monarch is considered a serious transgression.

When reciting *Shemoneh Esrei*, we are literally standing in Hashem's Presence. During this time, we must take special care to adhere to the protocol of His royalty and not add onto His praise. Deviation from this rule is considered a slight to His honor.

Limiting one's praises of Hashem applies primarily to *Shemoneh Esrei*, where we are forbidden to change the wording laid down by our Sages who established it. When it comes to personal requests that come from the heart, however, it is permitted to mention other praises of Hashem. Nonetheless, in order to avoid the above issues, it is preferable to limit one's praises to reciting verses from *Tehillim* or other sections of *Tanach* (*Shulchan Aruch* 113,9).

Second Blessing: Take Three | TUESDAY

"You are eternally mighty my Master, the Resuscitator of the dead are You, abundantly to save. He provides for the living with kindness, resuscitates the dead with great mercy, supports the fallen, heals the sick, frees the confined, and sustains His faith to those who sleep in the ground. Who is like You, Master of mightiness, and who can be compared to You, King who causes death and restores life and makes salvation blossom. And You are faithful to resuscitate the dead. Blessed are You Hashem, Who resuscitates the dead."

In the first blessing, we express Hashem's greatness. Although He owns the entire universe, He does not hesitate to remember the actions of our forefathers, who sanctified His Name in the world. In order to reward their devotion, He showers their offspring with innumerable acts of kindness, and will eventually bring them the final redemption.

The second blessing describes Hashem's power. The ultimate example of this is His control over life, as seen through His sustenance of the entire world and resurrection of the dead. During the winter, we add a praise for the rains, which play a major role in sustaining life.

Finally, in the third blessing, we make reference to His awe. Hashem is completely separate from this world, yet His holiness permeates every aspect of creation. During the days between Rosh Hashana and Yom Kippur, we recognize that His connection to this world is more apparent, by adding the word *King* to the conclusion of this blessing.

National Honor | WEDNESDAY

When we speak to Hashem in *Shemoneh Esrei*, we follow the pattern that applies when speaking to a human monarch. One initiates the conversation with praises of the king, followed by his requests. Before parting from the king, a person concludes with words of thanks (*Brachos* 34a).

In the course of the thirteen middle blessings of *Shemoneh Esrei*, a person may add personal requests. His requests should match up with the pertinent blessing. One should not make personal requests amidst the first three and last three blessings of *Shemoneh Esrei*, since they are dedicated to praising and thanking Hashem (*Shulchan Aruch* 112,1).

Some communities have the custom to say *piyutim* in the first blessings of *Shemoneh Esrei* (*Rema*, ibid.). However, since these *piyutim* contain national requests and are a deviation from the themes of the first three blessings, Sephardic communities do not recite them (*Shulchan Aruch* 112,2). Why do these requests differ from others?

The permissibility of *piyutim* containing national requests is analogous to the approach to human royalty. While it would be undignified for an individual to come before the king and immediately present personal requests, requests made on behalf of an entire nation are consistent with the monarch's dignity. They are a sign of honor, because they demonstrate that this king is both powerful and sought after. Therefore, these *piyutim* are permitted in the first and last sections of our *Shemoneh Esrei* (*Mishna Berura* 112,2).

The Book of Life | THURSDAY

From Rosh Hashana until Yom Kippur, we make a number of additions in the first and last sections. We ask Hashem to inscribe us for life, sustenance and everything else we need for a successful year. As explained earlier, since we are asking on behalf of the entire Jewish people, these requests are permitted in the first and last three blessings of *Shemoneh Esrei*.

If a person forgets one of these additions and remembers his omission before saying Hashem's Name, he should go back and repeat the blessing. Otherwise, he should continue *Shemoneh Esrei*. Since these prayers constitute additional praise, if one leaves them out completely he does not need to repeat *Shemoneh Esrei*. (*Mishna Berura* 582,16). However, if one forgets to say *Hamelech Hakadosh*, "the Holy King," in the third blessing he must repeat *Shemoneh Esrei*.

What should one do if he accidentally mentions these additions during other times of the year? If he has not finished the current blessing of *Shemoneh Esrei*, he should return to the place were he erred and repeat it without the superfluous words. Otherwise, he should complete *Shemoneh Esrei* without any changes (*Mishna Berura* 104,21).

Third Blessing: Burning Angels | FRIDAY

"You are holy and Your Name is holy, and holy ones praise You every day, forever. Blessed are You, Hashem, the holy G-d."

Prayer should be a mortifying experience. We stand before Hashem, Who is so exalted that no creature can possibly fathom or express His praise. How can we possibly meet this challenge and properly describe His greatness?

In the third blessing of *Shemoneh Esrei* we mention that *kedoshim* praise Hashem every day. During the *Kedusha*, recited during the repetition of *Shemoneh Esrei*, we make mention of some of these *kedoshim* - the *Seraphim*, burning angels. These Divine messengers have such a clear perception of G-d's power that they are constantly set into flame as a result. Obviously, we are not meant to copy their behavior.

On the other hand, we often take the opposite approach. We have already resigned ourselves to our inability to concentrate during *tefilla*, and rush through *Shemoneh Esrei* while our minds are occupied with other matters. How can we strike a balance between these two extremes?

During *Shemoneh Esrei* we are meant to look beyond ourselves. For at least five minutes, we are meant to be completely focused on Hashem and the Jewish people. For this reason none of the blessings is written in the singular.

Herein lies the secret to successful prayer. Before starting *Shemoneh Esrei*, we should remove ourselves from the picture and think only about Hashem and His people. During the first three blessings of *Shemoneh Esrei,* the recognition that His grandeur is the single source of strength in the universe should help us focus on the rest of our prayers. This thought will lift us above the level of the *Seraphim* and elevate our *tefilla* to the highest level.

We can attain the highest level
of praise during prayer
by focusing on Hashem's greatness
and forgetting about ourselves.

Personal Needs

Understanding the Middle Blessings of Shemoneh Esrei - Part One

Knowing What to Ask For | SHABBOS

The Roman General Vespasian was sent to conquer Jerusalem. After a long siege of the city, the inhabitants were beginning to weaken from hunger and fatigue, and it seemed that Vespasian was on the cusp of triumph. At that time, Rav Yochanan ben Zakai covertly left the walls of Jerusalem and sought a meeting with the Roman general.

Rav Yochanan greeted Vespasian as king, citing a verse that the Temple could be conquered only by royalty. Vespasian was initially offended by Rav Yochanan's seeming slight to the real monarch, but just then a messenger arrived from Rome and proclaimed that he had been appointed the new emperor. In order to reward Rav Yochanan for prophetically being the first to address him by his proper title, Vespasian offered to grant the great Sage a wish. Rav Yochanan then made his famous request, "Give me Yavneh and its Sages."

The Talmud takes issue with Rav Yochanan ben Zakai's

In memory of our parents
Norman and Sylvia Lieberman (Nahum Ben Chaim and Sheva bat Baruch)
From Barry and Frank Lieberman

request. At that moment of grace, when he could have asked for anything, shouldn't he have appealed that Jerusalem and the Temple not be destroyed? The Talmud cites the verse, "I am Hashem … that turns wise men backwards and makes their knowledge foolish" (*Isaiah* 44,25) to show that at times Hashem does not allow a person to ask for the right thing (*Gittin* 56b).

This story sends a strong message: We need Divine guidance in making important requests. And what requests could be more important than those we present daily before the King of kings during *Shemoneh Esrei*? Let us explore how the middle blessings of the *Shemoneh Esrei* guide a Jew to ask for the right things that he truly needs for himself and his family.

The Fourth Blessing:
Give Us the Wisdon to Know How to Ask

"You graciously endow man with wisdom and teach insight to a frail mortal. Endow us graciously from Yourself with wisdom, insight and discernment. Blessed are You, Hashem, gracious Giver of wisdom."

A person may view prayer as an opportunity to freely beg Hashem for whatever his heart desires. Yet from the Talmudic story, we learn that the act of opening our mouth in prayer requires Heavenly assistance to ensure that the appropriate words will emerge. Even when the great Sage stood in front of a king who was willing to grant any request, Hashem did not give him the wisdom to know what to ask and he did not make the most of that opportunity.

Atah chonen, the fourth blessing of *Shemoneh Esrei,* was composed with the above concept in mind. Prayer gives us the chance to ask Hashem for what we want, and we can easily squander this opportunity by asking for the wrong thing. Before starting to ask for our personal needs, we must first beg Hashem to give us enough understanding to know what we should ask for (*Shulchan Aruch* 115,1).

Since our Sages set down the precise wording for each request of the *Shemoneh Esrei* long ago, we may wonder why we are worried about asking for the right things. The answer is that even with the firm guidance of the words printed in the *siddur,* we still need assistance from Above. If we don't recognize that these blessings are exactly what we need, we will not put our heart into our prayers and we will not add personal requests in places where they are permitted.

Another insight comes from the words of our Sages, who tell us: "It is forbidden to have mercy on someone who does not have understanding" (*Brachos* 33a). Helping someone who will squander or abuse our assistance is a waste of resources. Therefore, before turning to Hashem for our other requests, we ask Him for the understanding that will help us to use His gifts properly and thus be worthy of receiving more (*Birkei Yosef* 115).

"Bring us back, our Father, to Your Torah, and bring us near, our King, to Your service, and influence us to return in perfect repentance before You. Blessed are You, Hashem, Who desires repentance."

Even if we had the wisdom to know exactly what to ask for, there still exist many obstacles that could prevent us from receiving what we need. Our Sages tell us that the greatest obstacles to the acceptance of our prayers are transgressions, which create a barrier between us and Hashem and block the flow of His bounty. In the fifth blessing of *Shemoneh Esrei*, we ask Hashem to help us repent so that we may receive all the gifts that He wishes to bestow upon us.

The fifth blessing, *Hashivenu*, contains three requests. We ask Hashem to bring us back to His Torah, to draw us close to His service, and to return us in complete repentance. However, we conclude the blessing by mentioning only repentance.

This same pattern is common to many of the other blessings of *Shemoneh Esrei*. We start with three requests and conclude with only one. What is the significance of this model?

Before we can to return to Hashem, we must first come back to His Torah and His service. Only through immersion in Torah and His service can we overcome the temptations for transgression and begin to tear down the barriers between us and our Maker that we have created through our wrongdoings. Therefore, we preface our main request for repentance with a plea to draw us closer to Torah and His service.

In all of the blessings based on this model, the first two things are essential prerequisites for the fulfillment of our primary, final request.

The Sixth Blessing: Complete Forgiveness | MONDAY

"Forgive us, our Father, for we have erred; pardon us, our King, for we have willfully sinned; for You pardon and forgive. Blessed are You, Hashem, the Gracious One who pardons abundantly."

The sixth blessing of *Shemoneh Esrei* is *Selach lanu*, in which we ask for complete forgiveness. We beg Hashem to wipe away our misdeeds, and pardon the dishonor we caused Him by transgressing His will. In doing so, we hope to do away with any barriers between us, so that nothing will prevent us from receiving His kindness.

"A king may not forgo his honor, but a father may forgo his honor" (*Kesubos* 17a). In both this blessing and the previous one, we address Hashem as our Father before calling Him our King. In doing so we hope that Hashem will focus on the father-child aspect of our relationship to Him, and overlook the dishonor to Him caused by our actions (*Beis Yosef* 115).

While saying the word "*selach*," we should think about any

specific transgression we may have done that day, and turn to Hashem in repentance. Some have the custom to tap twice on the area of their hearts with their fists, once when saying the word "*chatanu*" and once when saying "*pashanu.*" This gesture reminds us of *vidui*, confession, and helps arouse one's heart to repentance while reciting these words.

On days when *Tachanun* is not recited (e.g. *Rosh Chodesh* or *chol hamo'ed*), one should not tap the chest while saying this blessing. Since this gesture resembles *vidui*, it is improper to do so on happy days when *vidui* is not said (*Shelah*, as cited in *Siddur Yavetz*; Rav Shlomo Zalman Auerbach, as cited in *Halichos Shlomo* 11,45). Some authorities maintain that one should not tap the chest during evening services either, since *Tachanun* is not said at night (*Shaarei Halacha U'Minhag, Orach Chaim* 69).

The Seventh Blessing: Please Hear Our Pleas | TUESDAY

"Behold our difficulties, take up our grievance, and redeem us speedily for Your Name's sake, for You are a powerful Redeemer. Blessed are You, Hashem, Redeemer of Israel."

In the seventh, eighth and ninth blessings of *Shemoneh Esrei*, we ask Hashem to provide for our specific personal needs. We ask Him to spare us from hardship, sickness and poverty so that we may serve Him with peace of mind.

The seventh blessing is *Re'ei b'anyeinu*, and concludes with a plea for redemption. We also mention redemption in the tenth, eleventh and fifteenth blessings (*Takah b'shofar, Hashiva shofteinu,* and *Es tzemach David*). While the later blessings refer to redemption on a national level, in the seventh blessing one asks to be relieved of the private difficulties and suffering he endures in his own life of exile (*Rashi, Megilla* 17b).

Many halachic authorities maintain that the correct wording of this blessing is "*Re'ei na b'anyeinu,*" ("Please behold our difficulties") (*Rambam, Magen Avraham, Mishna Berura* 116,1). However, a number of earlier authorities determined that the word *please* should be omitted, based on the verse, "Look upon my affliction and pain" (*Tehillim* 25,18), which does not include the word *please* (*Responsa of the Rosh* 4,20; *Responsa of the Maharshal*, 64).

Generally, the Torah encourages politeness, and Yaakov Avinu is praised for always saying "please" (*Rashi, Toldos* 27,22). In this blessing, however, there is reason to leave it out. By omitting this formality, we emphasize that until the final redemption comes, we are in such a state of anguish that we cannot even muster up the strength to add "please" to our pleas.

The Eighth Blessing: Divine Healing |

"Heal us, Hashem – then we will be healed; save us – then we will be saved, for You are our praise. Bring complete recovery for all our ailments, for You are G-d, King, the faithful and compassionate Healer. Blessed are You, Hashem, Who heals the sick of His people Israel."

The eighth blessing of *Shemoneh Esrei* is *Refa'einu*, asking Hashem for health. A person can insert a prayer in the middle of this blessing for his own or another's recovery. Although a man is called up to the Torah as the child of his father, the Zohar writes that in prayer one should be referred to as the child of one's mother (*Zohar, Lech Lecha* 84).

Can a person mention the name of any sick person in *Shemoneh Esrei*? Rav Shlomo Zalman Auerbach maintained that a person should be closely associated with the people for whom he is praying, and it is improper to make requests for people with whom he has little or no connection during this blessing. Rav Shlomo Zalman would mention family members during the blessing of *Refa'einu* and others during the blessing of *Shema Koleinu* (*Halichos Shlomo* 15,60).

At times, a person is so sick that the doctors say there is no chance of survival. Some authorities write that upon reaching such a critical state, one is asking for an open miracle, and it is improper to pray for the patient (Rav Akiva Eiger, *Shulchan Aruch* 230 citing *Sefer HaChassidim* 795). Even at such a critical state, however, people should have complete confidence that Hashem has the power to effect healing, as the Talmud says that even if a sharp sword rests upon one's neck, one should never give up hope of Divine salvation (*Brachos* 10a).

The Ninth Blessing: Prosperity | THURSDAY

"Bless on our behalf – O Hashem, our G-d – this year and all its kinds of crops for the best and give (dew and rain for) a blessing on the face of the earth, and satisfy us from Your good, and bless our year like the best years. Blessed are You, Hashem, Who blesses the years."

The ninth blessing of *Shemoneh Esrei* is *Barech Aleinu*, asking Hashem for prosperity. Some versions say, "and satisfy us from Your good," while others read, "and satisfy us with its good." What is the significance of this distinction?

Although this part of *Shemoneh Esrei* is a prayer for general prosperity, it refers specifically to agricultural bounty. For this reason, some versions ask that we be satisfied from *its* good, referring to the land. We beg Hashem to bless the land so that it will produce an abundance of crops (Vilna Gaon on *Shulchan Aruch*).

However, prosperity is not necessarily equated with material abundance. If Hashem blesses the produce, then a person will be satisfied with even a small quantity. For this reason, some ask that we should be satisfied from *Your* blessing, referring to Hashem (*Responsa of the Rosh* 4,20 and *Responsa of Maharshal* 64).

Property and Prayer | FRIDAY

Requests for understanding, repentance, forgiveness, redemption, health and prosperity make up the personal requests of *Shemoneh Esrei*. Although we acknowledge on an intellectual level that each one of these requests is critical for our well-being at any given moment, we still have trouble stopping our minds from wandering during prayer. In today's fast-paced world, when we have so much on our minds, how can we focus on these requests day after day?

"Whoever wants to pray with concentration should work on treating his friend's property as carefully as his own" (*Kaf HaChaim* 98, 3 citing *Sefer HaMiddos* 2,10). At first glance, this advice may seem somewhat irrelevant. What is the connection between my prayer and another person's belongings?

Actually, this comment reveals a deep insight into the nature of prayer and the human condition. As mentioned in the previous section, one of the greatest challenges of standing before Hashem in prayer is to divert our attention from ourselves and our worldly cares and focus solely on our conversation with Hashem. As soon as we open our mouths, extraneous thoughts begin to pop into our minds and we must do constant battle to keep them at bay.

The essential characteristic of someone who is extremely careful with another's property is that he knows how to put someone other than himself first. He has mastered the self-control to put his own thoughts and desires aside for a period. When such an individual comes to say *Shemoneh Esrei*, he is ready to humble himself once again, and focus purely on his conversation with Hashem.

*We turn to Hashem
with our personal needs
in order to forge a
relationship with Him.*

14

Visions of Jerusalem

Understanding the Middle Blessings of Shemoneh Esrei - Part Two

Tears | SHABBOS

The story is told of Napoleon, who was walking one evening through the streets of Paris with his entourage when he happened to pass by a synagogue. From inside emerged the sounds of large numbers of people weeping bitterly.

He inquired as to what the Jews were so upset about. His aide replied that they were mourning the destruction of their Temple.

"Their Temple was destroyed?" Napoleon asked. "How come I wasn't informed of this news?"

"Their Temple in Jerusalem was destroyed more than 1,700 years ago on this date," the aide explained.

Napoleon was amazed, and said, "A people that mourns the loss of their Temple for so long will surely survive to see it rebuilt."

Every Tisha B'Av we still sit on the floor and try to bring ourselves to tears over the destruction of the Temple. However, many Jews today find it difficult to muster the level of anguish demonstrated in the above famous story.

The middle seven blessings of *Shemoneh Esrei* recall the glory of the Temple and the tragedy of exile. The blessings come together to provide a vision of Jerusalem and describe a complete picture of what life will be like when the redemption comes.

The Tenth Blessing: Return | SUNDAY

"Sound the great shofar for our freedom, raise the banner to gather our exiles and gather us together from the four corners of the earth. Blessed are You, Hashem, Who gathers in the dispersed of His people Israel."

In the ideal vision, all the Jewish people are living in the Land of Israel. The tenth blessing of *Shemoneh Esrei* asks Hashem for the fulfillment of this. Since this process will be heralded by the blast of a *shofar*, we mention it at the start of this blessing (*Tur* 118).

Some versions of this blessing add the word *"meheira,"* quickly, while some omit it (*Shaarei Teshuva* 118,1). Ashkenazim usually omit it, while other versions include it. Both wordings are halachically acceptable.

Some halachic authorities suggest a special reason to add the word *quickly* to this blessing. Hashem has already promised us that he will gather in all the Jews from exile, a process that we have seen beginning in our own times, so we do not need to ask for this. However, we do need to beg Hashem to fulfill this promise quickly and soon, and without the difficulties that our Sages say may accompany it (*Leket HaKemach HaChadash* 118,4, based on the *Chasam Sofer*).

Those who omit the word *quickly* from this blessing can rely on an alternative explanation. Although the ingathering of exiles has been promised, we fear that it will come with a terrible price of infighting and divisiveness among the Jewish people. We therefore ask that we should be gathered "together," and that the Jewish people should be unified in this process.

The Eleventh Blessing: Justice | MONDAY

"Restore our judges as in earliest times and our counselors as at first, remove from us sorrow and groan, and reign over us – You, Hashem, alone – with kindness and compassion and justify us through judgment. Blessed are You, Hashem, the King Who loves righteousness and judgment."

The eleventh blessing of *Shemoneh Esrei* asks for the return of Torah-based government. It follows the blessing for the ingathering of the exiles, for when this takes place all Jews will be judged by Torah law in the court of the *Sanhedrin* (*Megilla* 17b).

According to general halacha, any blessing that does not acknowledge the kingship of Hashem as "*Melech HaOlam*," is not a blessing (*Shulchan Aruch* 214,1). And yet almost all the blessings of *Shemoneh Esrei* omit this reference to kingship. Only the first blessing, which praises Hashem as great, powerful and awesome, which are all attributes of majesty, follows this rule, albeit indirectly (*Tosfos, Brachos* 40b). However, since the *Shemoneh Esrei* is one prayer, the connection of the subsequent blessings to the first one links them all to the acknowledgement of Hashem's Kingship (*Tur* 113).

The one exception to this rule is the eleventh blessing, which concludes: "the King Who loves righteousness and judgment." Some versions, in fact, leave out the word *King* (see *Tur* 118); however, most *siddurim* include it.

From Rosh Hashana until Yom Kippur everyone changes the wording of this blessing to "the King of judgment." If an Ashkenazi unthinkingly says the regular formula he has still fulfilled his obligation, since he has said the word *King*. During the Ten Days of Repentance we focus on acknowledging Hashem's kingship in the world, and one can accomplish this through either version (*Rema* 118,1).

The Twelfth Blessing: Heretics | TUESDAY

"And for slanderers let there be no hope; and may all evil perish in an instant; and may all Your enemies be cut down speedily. May You speedily uproot, smash, cast down and humble the wanton sinners – speedily in our days. Blessed are You, Hashem, Who breaks enemies and humbles wanton sinners."

The twelfth blessing of *Shemoneh Esrei* asks Hashem to destroy heretics. It follows the previous blessing, for after a Torah government is restored, the time will come when all heretics, who deny and seek to destroy the Torah, will be put in their place (*Megilla* 17b). This blessing was not part of the original formulation of the *Shemoneh Esrei*, but was added by the Sages at a later time.

The Talmud tells us that when Rabbi Meir prayed that the evil people should be destroyed, his wife Bruriah corrected him that it was preferable to ask Hashem to have them return to the right path. The Zohar writes that it is forbidden to ask Hashem to destroy evil people (*Medrash Nelam, Vayera*). In light of this, why are we permitted to recite this blessing?

In general, one ought to pray that evil people should return to Hashem, and not be killed. However, the Torah makes an exception for heretics, whose goal in life is to trivialize, deny and eradicate the Torah. It is to these individuals whom we refer when we ask, "May all evil perish in an instant."

With regards to other evil people, the halacha upholds Bruriah's opinion, and one should definitely pray that they return to Hashem. Notwithstanding the general principle that, "Everything is in the hands of Heaven except the fear of Heaven," we may pray that everyone will return to the right path. Our intention should be that the evil should not be tempted to engage in further sin, and that they should meet righteous individuals who may help them find fear of Heaven once more (Rav Moshe Feinstein, as cited in *Responsa Rivavos Ephraim* 3,591).

The Thirteenth Blessing: Righteous People | WEDNESDAY

"On the righteous, on the devout, on the elders of Your people the Family of Israel, on the remnant of their scholars, on the righteous converts and on ourselves ... Put our lot with them forever, and we will not feel ashamed, for we trust in You. Blessed are You, Hashem, mainstay and assurance of the righteous."

The thirteenth blessing of *Shemoneh Esrei* refers to the righteous. It follows the previous blessing, for after the destruction of the heretics the righteous will regain their true stature (*Megilla* 17b).

The *Medrash* relates that someone once slandered a certain righteous rabbi. Afterwards, the speaker was surprised to receive a present from the rabbi with the following note attached to it:

"By speaking negatively about me, you caused me to receive all of the reward for your mitzvos. Since you gave me a present, I am sending you one as well!"

When saying the words, "and our portion should be with the righteous," we should keep the above thought in mind. If our portion in the World to Come has been forfeited due to our transgressions, Hashem should allow us to repent and get it back, so that when we get to the World to Come we should also have a place there with the righteous (*Arizal*, as cited in *Kaf HaChaim* 117,5).

The Fourteenth Blessing: Jerusalem and Redemption
THURSDAY

"And to Jerusalem, Your city, may You return in compassion, and may You rest within it, as You have spoken. May You rebuild it soon in our days as an eternal structure, and may You speedily establish the throne of David within it. Blessed are You, Hashem, the builder of Jerusalem."

The fourteenth blessing of *Shemoneh Esrei* asks Hashem to rebuild Jerusalem. It follows the blessing for the reward of the righteous, for when Jerusalem returns to its original splendor the righteous will once again be raised to their rightful status (*Megilla* 17b).

As a general rule, every long blessing reiterates its theme

before its conclusion. In this blessing, we finish with a request that King David's throne should be speedily established. How does this request fit into the above rule?

In our own era, we have been privileged to see the physical rebuilding and resettling of Jerusalem. Unfortunately, it is still a far cry from the Torah's vision of the Holy City. The wording of this blessing stresses the undying connection between the return of the kingship of David and the true rebuilding of Jerusalem (*Bach* 118,2).

The Fifteenth Blessing: Moshiach | FRIDAY

"The offspring of Your servant David may You speedily cause to flourish, and enhance his pride through Your salvation, for we hope for Your salvation all day long. Blessed are You, Hashem, Who causes the pride of salvation to flourish."

The fifteenth blessing of *Shemoneh Esrei* asks for the coming of the Moshiach. After asking Hashem to rebuild Jerusalem, we ask for the completion of the final redemption with the crowning of David's descendent as Moshiach and king of Israel.

Our Sages tell us that, upon leaving this world, we will be asked six questions. One of them will be, "Did you yearn for redemption?" (*Shabbos* 31a). According to the Arizal, when we recite the fifteenth blessing, we should allow ourselves to experience yearning for redemption in order that we may reply affirmatively when asked this question (*Shaar Hakavanos*). The Zohar notes that someone who does not yearn for the final redemption in this world, will not have a place in the World to Come (*Introduction to Bereishis* 4a).

On a personal level, every person faces challenges each day, be they major or minor. While saying this blessing, we should keep in mind that one of the reasons that Hashem is sending us these trials is so that we will ask Him to help us, in fulfillment of the blessing that "We hope for Your salvation all day long" (*Kaf HaChaim* 119,8 citing *Chida*).

The Sixteenth Blessing: Hear Our Prayer

"Hear our voice, Hashem our G-d, pity and be compassionate to us, and accept – with compassion and favor – our prayer, for You are G-d Who hears prayers and supplications. Do not turn us away empty-handed from before Yourself, our King, for You hear the prayers of Your people Israel with compassion. Blessed are You, Hashem, Who hears prayers."

In the second half of *Shemoneh Esrei*, we ask for the ingathering of the exiles and the return of Torah rule, the downfall of the evil and the rise of the righteous, the rebuilding of Jerusalem and the return of the kingship of David. It would seem that these blessings come together to create a perfect picture of what Jews are praying for on a national level. Yet after nearly 2,000 years, we have still not been answered. What can we do so that our prayers will at last be fulfilled?

Our situation can be likened to a man in trouble, who was given an audience with a high-ranking official. The distressed man explained his problem and asked the official to exert his influence in order to help him. But his request fell on deaf ears, and the official seemed poised to send him away empty-handed.

In a final burst of desperation, the man broke down and tearfully begged the official to find it in his heart to help him. Unable to remain unmoved in the face of this sincere display of emotion, the official agreed to help.

The sixteenth blessing of *Shemoneh Esrei* is this last-ditch plea. We turn to Hashem with an emotional cry to hear the urgency in our voice, and finally grant us that for which we begged Him so many times. If we can muster up the true desire in our heart for that which we request, we will surely be answered quickly.

There is always a danger in taking such an approach. The listener may be temporarily moved to comply with what we ask, but later on may feel that he was manipulated into doing something against his will. For this reason we ask Hashem to accept our prayers with both compassion and favor, in order that our requests should not strain our relationship with Him.

The words of Shemoneh Esrei
paint a picture of
how the Jewish people
are meant to be.

15

Self-Sacrifice

Understanding the Last Three Blessings of Shemoneh Esrei

Burnt Offerings | SHABBOS

During the era of the Roman domination of Israel, the Sage Rebbi Yossi ben Kisma fell sick, and Rebbi Chanina ben Tradion went to visit him.

Rebbi Yossi asked Rebbi Chanina, "Chanina, don't you know that this nation was chosen from Above to rule over us, destroy the *Beis Hamikdash*, burn its sanctuary, kill its righteous ones, and wipe out its good people? So why am I hearing that you are publicly teaching Torah and you keep a *sefer Torah* with you?"

"From the Heavens they will have mercy on me," responded Rebbi Chanina.

"I'm offering you advice and you tell me that from Heaven they will have mercy on you!" replied Rebbi Yossi. "I wouldn't be surprised if they burn you together with your *sefer Torah*!"

"[If they kill me] will I merit entering the World to Come?" asked Rebbi Chanina.

L'zeicher Nishmas
**Zev ben Yosef, Mordechai ben Reuven, Rashka bas Gedalayahu,
Tzvi ben Aryeh, Esther bas Dove Berish**
From the Newman Family

"Have you done anything to merit a place there?" questioned Rebbi Yossi.

Rebbi Chanina thought for a moment and responded, "Once money that I had saved for my family's Purim meal got mixed up with *tzedaka* money I was holding. I gave all the money to poor people and did not take any compensation back from the *tzedaka*."

"Since you gave up your own money to *tzedaka*," concluded Rebbi Yossi, "you will receive a place in the World to Come with me."

It was not long before Rebbi Yossi ben Kisma died, and all of the leaders of Rome came to participate in the funeral and eulogize him. On their way home they saw Rebbi Chanina ben Tradion teaching Torah publicly from a *sefer Torah*. They wrapped the Torah scroll around him and set it on fire.

The Romans placed pads of wet wool around his heart so that his death throes would be prolonged. Rebbi Chanina's daughter saw him and said, "Father, I can't see you like this!" He replied, "If I was being burned alone, it would be difficult for me. But since I am being burned together with a *sefer Torah*, I know that He Who takes vengeance for the disgrace of the Torah will take vengeance for my death."

Kaltzanori, the person appointed by the Romans to guard Rebbi Chanina, asked him, "Rebbi, if I increase the fire and remove the wool from your heart so that you will die quicker, will I get a place in the World to Come?" Rebbi Chanina replied that he would. "Swear to me that this is so," pleaded Kaltzanori. Rebbi Chanina swore, and Kaltzanori brought more firewood and took off the wool. Rebbi Chanina died instantly, and Kaltzanori jumped into the fire.

A voice emanated from Heaven proclaiming, "Rebbi Chanina and Kaltzanori have earned a place in the World to Come!" When Rebbi Yehuda heard this, he cried and said, "Some people earn their portion in the world to come in one moment, while some people need many years" (*Avoda Zara* 18a).

Let us explore how this story of faith and martyrdom relates to the powerful final blessings of the *Shemoneh Esrei.*

The Seventeenth Blessing: Fires of Israel | SUNDAY

"Be favorable, Hashem, our G-d, toward Your people Israel and their prayer and restore the service to the Holy of Holies of Your Temple. The 'ishei Yisrael' and their prayer accept with love and favor."

The seventeenth blessing of *Shemoneh Esrei* begs Hashem to find the Jewish people and their service of Him favorable. Among the things that we ask Hashem to look favorably on are *ishei Yisrael*, which can be translated as either "the individuals of Israel" or the "fires of Israel."

The second translation refers to the countless Jewish people throughout the ages who have lost their lives as a sanctification of G-d's name, at the hands of oppressors who sought to wipe the Jews and the Torah off the face of the earth. Someone who is killed by fire, like Rabbi Chanina ben Tradion, is literally transformed into an *ishei Yisrael*, a human burnt offering (*Pikudei Eliezer,* as cited in the *Leket Hakemach HaChadash*).

Some explain that *ishei Yisrael* refers to the burnt offerings that were sacrificed in the Temple. A person bringing this offering was meant to recognize that, because of his transgressions, *he* deserved to be burnt up on the altar. When the person bringing the sacrifice understands that it is a substitute for himself, these burnt offerings are also considered *ishei Yisrael* (based on *Gra* 120,1, according to *Tosfos Menachos* 110a).

Ishei Yisrael can also refer to the souls of the Jewish people. The *Medrash* says that the angel Michael serves as the *kohen gadol* in the heavens, and after the righteous pass away, he brings their souls as a sacrifice before Hashem every day. We ask Hashem to favor the souls of these *ishei Yisrael* (*Taz,* according to *Tosfos Menachos* 110a).

All of the above explanations of *ishei Yisrael* share a common thread related to giving up something of ourselves to Hashem. Let us try to understand how each of the final blessings develops this theme.

"May the service of Your people Israel always be favorable to you. May our eyes merit to see Your return to Tzion in compassion. Blessed are You, Hashem, Who returns His Presence to Tzion."

On *chol hamo'ed* and *Rosh Chodesh*, festive sacrifices were brought in the Temple. We commemorate these offerings with the extra *Mussaf* prayer, as well as the special addition of the *yaleh v'yavo* passage to the seventeenth blessing of *Shemoneh Esrei*.

The general theme of this blessing is the Temple service. Since *yaleh v'yavo* replaces the additional sacrifices, our Sages felt it proper to insert it in this point of *Shemoneh Esrei*. It is said right before concluding the blessing.

At times, out of habit, a person might finish this blessing, having forgotten to insert *yaleh v'yavo*. As long as he has not started the next blessing, he can still recite *yaleh v'yavo* and then continue as usual.

If he realized the omission after starting the next blessing, he cannot just insert *yaleh v'yavo* at the point where he remembers. He must return to the start of the seventeenth blessing and say *yaleh v'yavo* in its proper place. If one already finished reciting *Shemoneh Esrei* by the time he notices, he must repeat the entire *Shemoneh Esrei*.

There is one exception to the above rule. If a person forgot to say *yaleh v'yavo* on the night of *Rosh Chodesh*, he does not go back and correct his error. Since in the times of the Temple the new month could not be proclaimed at night, if one accidentally leaves out *yaleh v'yavo* it does not disqualify his nighttime *Shemoneh Esrei* (*Shulchan Aruch* 222,1).

The Eighteenth Blessing: Expressing Gratitude | TUESDAY

"We gratefully acknowledge that You are Hashem, our G-d and the G-d of our forefathers for all eternity; Rock of our lives, Shield of our salvation are You from generation to generation. We shall thank You and relate Your praise – for our lives, which are committed to Your power and for our souls that are entrusted to You."

In addition to the burnt offerings, many different types of sacrifices were brought daily in the Temple. The *korban todah*, the thanksgiving offering, was brought in the times of the Temple to express one's gratitude to Hashem for special Divine Providence. Now that the Temple no longer stands, the eighteenth blessing of *Shemoneh Esrei*, *Modim*, helps take its place by thanking Hashem for the innumerable revealed and hidden miracles He performs for us each day.

"When the final redemption comes, sacrifices and prayers will be terminated, with the exception of the thanksgiving offering"

(*Vayikra Rabba* 9,7). At the end of days, there will be no more transgressions and there will no longer be a need for repentance sacrifices. However, we will continue to recognize Hashem's constant kindness by offering the *korban todah* and with prayers of thanks.

When the prayer leader repeats *Shemoneh Esrei,* we listen to all of the blessings from him. There is one exception: *Modim.* Since we can only offer proper thanks to Hashem by doing so ourselves, our Sages compiled a special prayer, *Modim D'rabbanan,* to be said while *Shemoneh Esrei* is repeated (*Abudaraham*).

The Eighteenth Blessing (cont.): For the Miracles | WEDNESDAY

"For Your miracles that are with us every day; and for Your wonders and favors at every season – evening, morning and afternoon. The Beneficent One, for Your compassions were never exhausted, and the Compassionate One, for Your kindnesses never ended – always have we put our hope in You ... Blessed are You, Hashem, Whose name is good and to Whom it is fitting to give thanks."

We thank Hashem for all of the miracles that He performs every day, evening, morning and afternoon. After praising Him for what He does every day, is it really necessary to mention these three different time periods? By enumerating these three different times we recognize that during every part of the day there are different miracles for which we need to thank Hashem.

During the stories of both Chanukah and Purim, it seemed as if the Jewish people were headed for spiritual and physical annihilation. In both cases Hashem performed miracles on our behalf, which caused the exact opposite to transpire, and the Jews had resounding victories over their enemies. On both Chanukah and Purim we recognize that in addition to the myriad of hidden miracles that He is constantly performing for us, at times we are privileged to recognize His hand in the world with open miracles. We do so by adding *Al Hanisim* to the eighteenth blessing of *Shemoneh Esrei*, describing the miracles that Hashem did for us "in those days at this time."

If one forgot to say *Al Hanisim* but did not yet say Hashem's Name, he can go back and say *Al Hanisim*. If he has already said Hashem's Name he should continue, and he does not need to recite *Shemoneh Esrei* again; rather, he should insert *Al Hanisim* at the end of *Shemoneh Esrei* before taking three steps back. Instead of saying the words "*Al Hanisim*" until "*b'zman hazeh*," he should preface his prayer with the words, "*Harachaman Hu yaseh lanu nisim v'nifla'os kemo she'asa lavoseinu bayamim hahem b'zman hazeh ...*" and then continue with the appropriate section for Purim or Chanukah (*Mishna Berura* 682,4).

The Nineteenth Blessing: Prayers of Peace | T H U R S D A Y

"Establish peace, goodness, blessing, graciousness, kindness and mercy upon us and all of Your people Israel ... May it be good in Your eyes to bless Your people Israel in every season and every hour with Your peace. Blessed are You, Hashem, Who blesses his people with peace."

In the nineteenth and final blessing of *Shemoneh Esrei*, *Sim Shalom,* we ask Hashem to grant us peace. Just as *Birkas Kohanim*, the Priestly Blessing, ends with a blessing for peace, so too we conclude *Shemoneh Esrei* with a request for peace. Our Sages tell us, in fact, that all blessings end with a request for peace (*Yalkut Shimoni, Naso* 711).

According to some early commentators, each person should mention the words of *Birkas Kohanim* in their silent *Shemoneh Esrei* before saying the nineteenth blessing (*Kol Bo* and *Maharil*, as cited in *Prisha* 121,5). We do not follow this practice, and only say *Birkas Kohanim* (or a substitute prayer) during the repetition of *Shemoneh Esrei.*

There is a strong connection between *Birkas Kohanim* and the nineteenth blessing that follows it. During *Birkas Kohanim* we make six requests: that Hashem should bless us, guard us, enlighten us, show us grace, lift us up and grant us peace.

In the blessing of *Sim Shalom* we ask for the fulfillment of these six requests of *Birkas Kohanim*. We ask Hashem for peace, good, blessing, grace, kindness and mercy (*Elia Rabba*

127,6). For this reason, many have the custom only to recite *Sim Shalom* in the morning of a normal weekday or in the afternoon of a fast day when *Birkas Kohanim* is said, and at other times say *Shalom Rav* (*Mishna Berura* 127,12).

The Nineteenth Blessing (cont.): Tranquility through Torah | FRIDAY

In Israel, the custom of Ashkenazim is to start the final blessing of *Shemoneh Esrei* with the words "*Sim Shalom*" rather than "*Shalom Rav*" on Shabbos afternoon. The reason for this is that we read from the Torah, which is hinted to by the words "*or panecha*" ("the light of Your face") in this blessing (*Rema* 127,2). This halacha implies a connection between peace and Torah.

"Hashem gave His strength [i.e. the Torah] to Israel, Hashem will bless His people with peace" (*Tehillim* 29,11). Similarly, the *medrash* says that when the Jewish people said, "*Na'aseh V'Nishma*," ("We will do and then we will hear") at the time of the giving of the Torah, Hashem blessed them with peace. What is the connection between peace and Torah?

"Torah scholars increase peace in the world ..." (*Brachos* 64a). *Talmidei chachamim* are so engrossed in understanding Hashem's will that they forget about their own desires. Such a person acquires the habit of putting the will of another before his own, a trait which fosters peace in every relationship.

When the great Torah scholar Rav Shlomo Zalman Auerbach's wife passed away, he forewent the general custom to ask forgiveness from the deceased. He explained: "We lived our lives according to the Torah. During the course of fifty years of marriage, we never had an argument."

Most of us will not reach the exalted level of Rav and Rebbetzin Auerbach. However, if we remember that the goal of both prayer and Torah study is to learn to align our own will with that of our Creator's, we are already on the way to achieving true and everlasting peace.

As we prepare to leave
Hashem's Presence,
we offer the ultimate sacrifice
to Hashem – ourselves.

16

Leaving the King

Understanding the Three Steps Back after Shemoneh Esrei

Until the Last Moment | SHABBOS

During the early 1900s poverty in Eastern Europe was so dire that many Jews were on the verge of starvation. Countless men left the shtetl behind and traveled to America in search of a job that could bring some relief to their families. On the day of a person's departure, friends and family would accompany him to the train station to see him off.

When they arrived at the train station, the crowd would bid him farewell, except for close family, who would board the train and ride with him to the border. At the border everyone would say good-bye and return home, except for one person – his wife. She would continue on with him and delay their parting until the last possible moment – when he boarded the boat to America.

In Yiddish, they would say, *"Tzu shver shidden, nisht shidden"* – whoever has a hard time leaving, does not really leave. Even

L'zeicher Nishmas
Naftali ben Leah
Niftar on the 21st of Tevet

though husbands and wives would be separated for many years, many later testified that they remained close in their hearts. The final journey where the wife accompanied the husband until the last possible moment created a strong bond between them, which kept them attached for the coming years until they were finally reunited.

During *Shemoneh Esrei* we share such a moment of closeness with Hashem. At the conclusion of *Shemoneh Esrei,* when we take three steps backwards, we are given an opportunity to express our pangs of regret as we depart from His Presence. In doing so we create a bond that carries us through until the next time we meet.

These three steps backwards are one of the most critical moments of our prayers, so much so that our Sages say, "If one does not take these three steps, it is better that he should not have said *Shemoneh Esrei* at all" (*Yoma* 53b). Let us look into the halachos and customs of this special mitzva.

Leaving Hashem | SUNDAY

After reciting *Shemoneh Esrei*, one cannot simply stroll off. Our Sages set down exact guidelines showing us how to take leave of the Divine Presence. Studying them allows us to perform this mitzva in a way that bespeaks the honor due to our Creator.

In order to understand any area of Torah, one must first be familiar with the reasons for the halacha. There are many explanations offered for these three steps, but halachic authorities focus on two in particular. Numerous practical ramifications are derived from these two reasons.

Some write that *Shemoneh Esrei* is like the offering of the *Tamid* sacrifice and the one praying is like a *kohen* performing the Temple service (*Beis Yosef* citing Rav Hai Gaon). After offering the *Tamid*, the *kohen* would pour a wine libation onto the altar. The *kohen* would then exit by walking backwards, placing the toes of each foot behind the heel of his other foot (*Mor Uketzia* 123).

Others write that the steps back show that one is like a servant departing from his master (*Rashba, Responsa* 1,381). Before a servant leaves his master's presence, he bows down to show his humility and then walks backwards from the room. This shows that even as he gets ready to leave his master, he remains subservient to him and constantly alert for the moment when he will be summoned again (*Mishna Berura* 123,1).

Big and Small Steps | MONDAY

The size of the steps that one takes backwards depends on the reason for these steps. The first reason offered is that the person in prayer is like the *kohen* offering a sacrifice. According to this explanation, one steps backwards putting his toe behind his heel, since this was the way that the *kohanim* performed the Temple service (*Darchei Moshe* 123,2).

The second reason given for the steps is that the person in prayer is like a servant departing from his master. The Rema understands that, according to this reason, there is no minimum size of the steps, and even tiny ones are acceptable (*Darchei Moshe ibid.*). While we generally follow the first opinion, some halachic authorities rely on the other opinion and allow us to take smaller steps if there is limited space in the shul (*Mishna Berura* citing *Bach*).

Women did not participate in this service in the *Beis Hamikdash*; must they be careful about the size of their steps? Some authorities rule that women may rely on the second reason and take smaller steps (*Ishei Yisrael* 23,215 citing *Orach Ne'eman* 123,11). Others imply that the established halacha applies to men and women equally, and women must also be exact in the size of their steps (*Magen Avraham* 123,10).

The Rema warns that according to both views one should not take large steps backward (*ibid.*). Not only are these strides unfit for the Temple service, but they give the appearance that one is eager to run away from one's Master (*Mishna Berura* 123,16). The *Shulchan Aruch*, however, implies that one may take larger steps back (123,3).

Taking the Steps

According to both reasons, our Sages established these three steps as a way to show honor in our departure. The Zohar goes to great lengths to describe the deep significance of exactly how these steps are done, and how the directions that we bow correspond to different aspects of G-d's Presence (*Beis Yosef* 123). Even if these reasons may seem beyond our comprehension, they inspire us to recognize how important it is to take the steps properly.

While bowing, we take the first step backwards with our left foot (*Shulchan Aruch* 123,3). Although halacha generally gives preference to the right over the left, in this case since the right foot is generally more agile, by starting with the left we show that leaving prayer is difficult for us (*Mishna Berura* 123,13). Therefore, a lefty should take the first step backwards with his right foot (*Biur Halacha*).

We place the left foot behind the right one, taking a full step back. After moving the left foot back, we move the right foot behind the left one (i.e., the length of two feet). Finally, we complete our departure by bringing the left foot alongside the right one (*Mishna Berura* 123,13).

After we have finished our steps back, while still in a bowed position we turn left, bow and say, "*Oseh shalom bimromav*" ("He Who makes peace above"). We then turn right and say,

"*Hu ya'aseh shalom aleinu*" ("may He make peace upon us"). In conclusion, we bow forward and say, "*V'al kol Yisrael, v'imru amen* ("and on all of Israel, let us say *amen*") (*Shulchan Aruch* 123,1 and *Mishna Berura* 123: 3,5).

What should a person do if there is no room to take three steps backwards? In this situation he may take three steps to the side (*Aruch Hashulchan* 123,5). If even this is not possible, he can take very small steps backward (*Mishna Berura* 123,14).

Coming Back | WEDNESDAY

Some authorities rule that after taking three steps backward there is a mitzva to take three steps forward. Since when leaving *Shemoneh Esrei* one is like a servant departing from his master, it is very inappropriate to immediately take three steps forward (*Yoma* 53b). Instead he should wait until he has a good reason to return to where he was standing (*Mishna Berura* 123,7).

Therefore, if a person is praying together with a congregation he should wait until *Kedusha* or at night until *kaddish*. If it is difficult to wait that long, he should remain in the place where he finished his steps until the *shaliach tzibbur* starts his repetition of *Shemoneh Esrei* (*Shulchan Aruch* 123,2). If one is praying alone, one should pause for at least a few seconds before returning to one's place (*Rema ibid.*).

In his later years, the Brisker Rav had difficulty standing up until *Kedusha* after completing *Shemoneh Esrei* due to poor health. After he finished taking three steps back he would sit down in the place where he was. In this way he was able to fulfill the mitzva of not returning to his place right away.

Unusual Circumstances | THURSDAY

Rav Shlomo Zalman Auerbach was once asked how a person confined to a wheelchair should act in regards to the three steps back. He prefaced his answer commenting that the three steps backward are an integral part of one's prayer. Whatever circumstances a person finds himself in, he should make every effort to do them properly.

The halachic literature discusses a case of a person who is riding on a horse and cannot dismount to recite *Shemoneh Esrei*. He is permitted to say *Shemoneh Esrei* on his horse, and should fulfill the mitzva of taking three steps backwards by moving the animal backwards (*Rema* 94,5). In modern-day terms, if a person pulls to the side of the highway to recite *Mincha* and because of his circumstances must daven in his car, he should reverse the car backwards a distance of three steps after completing his *Shemoneh Esrei*.

Therefore, ruled Rav Auerbach, if possible the person in the wheelchair should try to move the chair backward the distance of three steps. If he is unable to accomplish this himself, he should ask someone else to move him. In this way, he will properly fulfill the mitzva (as cited in *Nishmas Avraham* 1: 123,2).

Some authorities rule that when traveling on a plane, bus or subway it is preferable to pray in one's seat. This situation makes taking three steps backwards difficult, for unlike riding on a horse or sitting in a wheelchair, the chair is fixed in place and cannot be moved backwards. Nonetheless, if a person is able to stand up to take these steps back at the end of his *Shemoneh Esrei*, he should do so (*Igros Moshe Orach Chaim* 4,20).

Protected from Harm | FRIDAY

"A person involved with a mitzva will not be harmed on the way to or from performing the mitzva" (*Pesachim* 8b). We can understand the importance of protection on the way to a mitzva – unless we get there, the mitzva will not be performed. Why do we merit additional safeguarding from danger on our return?

As we see from the conclusion of *Shemoneh Esrei*, the manner in which a person takes leave of another reflects his deeper feelings throughout the time they were together. If he runs away quickly, we can be sure that he did not cherish that time. However, if he has to pull himself away reluctantly, this shows that every minute was precious to him, and he is only leaving because the time has come to move on.

For this very reason, protective powers of the mitzva continue to safeguard a person even on his way back from performing it. The person's eagerness to perform the mitzva demonstrated how precious it was to him, and thus his departure is considered a continuation of his attachment to Hashem.

Through three slow and deliberate steps back at the end of *Shemoneh Esrei*, we show our true feelings of closeness to Hashem, even though our concentration may not have been exemplary throughout the prayer. In this way, the protective powers of the mitzva and our bond with Hashem will remain with us until our next meeting.

"Tzu shver shidden,

nisht shidden" –

Whoever has a hard time leaving,

does not really leave.

17

Finishing Touches

Understanding the End of Shemoneh Esrei

The Power of Prayer | SHABBOS

Rav Yosef of Ampalia was a devoted servant of Hashem and was known to recite *Shemoneh Esrei* with intense fervor. One day he fell seriously ill; he became extremely pale and his breathing slowed down. His attendants were unsure whether his soul had already departed from this world. Moments later he began to regain his color, and eventually he returned to full health. When asked what had transpired during those moments where he seemed suspended between life and death, he related the following:

Rav Yosef saw his soul being brought before the Heavenly Court, together with all of the prayers he had recited. Suddenly a *malach* came and asked, "What are all of these prayers doing here?" and blew them all away, with the exception of one letter: *hei*.

1 8 4   In memory of my grandparents **Reuven ben Shraga, Rivka bas Reuven, Zusman ben Pinchas, Perel bas Avraham**, and in memory of all my relatives who perished al Kiddush Hashem in the Shoah.
Eliyahu ben Shraga Starr

At that moment there was a funeral of a *tzaddik* taking place, and the souls of all the righteous came down from heaven to greet the new arrival. One of those who came to greet the soul was Rabbi Yisrael ben Eliezer, the rabbi of Rav Yosef of Ampalia. When he saw his student standing in judgment before the Heavenly Court he asked, "What is he doing here? Do you know how much fervor he puts into his prayers?"

In order to lend credence to his plea, the Heavenly Court allowed Rav Yosef to recite *Shemoneh Esrei* before Hashem. His prayer was filled with such passion that it lifted up all of his other prayers that had been blown away. As a result his soul was allowed to return to its body (as cited in *Taamei Haminhagim* p. 51).

When we get to the final stages of *Shemoneh Esrei*, we might think that our chance for a focused and passionate prayer has passed, and perhaps has been missed. From the story of Rav Yosef we see that it is never too late to inject the fervor necessary to lift up all of one's previous prayers. After the nineteen blessings are concluded, we are given another chance to storm the Heavens, with the paragraph "*Elokai Natzor.*"

Slander and Falsehood |

The conclusion of *Shemoneh Esrei* begins with the words: "Hashem, guard my tongue from evil and my lips from deceitful words." Of all the requests we could make at that auspicious moment, what is the significance of this one?

Our Sages tells us that debasing one's lips with words of slander and falsehood could cause one's prayers to go unanswered. Therefore, as soon as we finish *Shemoneh Esrei*, the first thing we do is ask Hashem to guard us from forbidden speech. By declaring our utter disdain for any form of untruth, we hope that all our prayers will find favor.

King David developed this idea further in *Tehillim* when he wrote, "Guard your tongue from evil, and your lips from deceitful words ... The eyes of G-d are upon the righteous, and His ears are open to their prayers. They cry out and G-d hears, and He rescues them from all their troubles" (34: 13,15). From the juxtaposition of these verses, King David's message is clear: One who guards his speech will see the fruits of his effort – his prayers will be answered! For this reason, this plea is perfectly placed at the conclusion of all of our prayers during *Shemoneh Esrei*.

Protection from Enemies | MONDAY

After asking Hashem to protect us from impure speech, we continue with a number of petitions. Although we ask for many things in this prayer, two are especially noteworthy. First, we address those who curse us. Instead of throwing it back at them, we ask that those that want to curse us should be quieted.

Afterwards, we address those who think evil against us. Instead of wishing bad upon our enemies, we ask Hashem that He should quickly overturn their plans and disrupt their thoughts. These strategies protect us from our enemies without causing them any harm, and teach us the Torah approach in dealing with those who seek to harm us.

Although we generally do not make personal requests on Shabbos, we make an exception by reciting this passage at the end of *Shemoneh Esrei*. Since *Elokai Natzor* is recited the same way every day, it is not covered by the prohibition against making personal requests on Shabbos (*Pri Chadash* 122,1).

Personal Requests | TUESDAY

Halachic authorities note that this point of prayer is an auspicious time to make personal requests on weekdays. A special emphasis should be placed on the prayer that one's children succeed in learning and fulfilling the mitzvos, and that one receives the livelihood he needs. These private prayers can be said in any language, with the only requirement being that they come from the heart (*Mishna Berura* 122,8).

During our first year of marriage, my wife and I faced an unusually large number of challenging circumstances. We asked Harav Shlomo Brevda for guidance, and he assured us that under such circumstances, prayer was the only solution. He advised us to ask for salvation from the specific difficulties that we were undergoing at the conclusion of *Shemoneh Esrei*, and to conclude our personal prayers with the following words:

"Even though I am not worthy to ask for such requests, nonetheless please do not turn me away empty-handed from before You, for I am pleading to You with a broken heart, and on Your tremendous kindness and Your incredible mercy I put all of my trust. May my heart rejoice in Your salvation."

We took Rav Brevda's words to heart and said this *tefilla* every weekday at the end of *Shemoneh Esrei* of *Shacharis* and *Mincha*. Within a short time, our situation changed dramatically for the better.

What's In a Name? | WEDNESDAY

At the end of this passage, some have a custom to mention a verse which begins with the first letter and ends with the last letter of their name. What is the deeper meaning behind this practice?

The Zohar writes that after a person's soul is taken from this world, he will be brought before the Heavenly Court and will be asked his name. To the embarrassment of many, they will not be able to answer this seemingly simple question. Considering that we hear our names so frequently throughout life, why won't we be able to answer this question on the final day of judgment?

A person's name represents his purpose in this world. A person who devoted his entire life to seeking out and fulfilling his purpose will have no difficulty in answering this question. For those of us who may have been distracted from this goal at times, how can we ensure that we will remember our name?

There is no greater expression of a Jew's individuality than his prayer. By signing off our *tefillos* with verses that allude to our names in this world, we stamp our prayers with our identities. This powerful *segula* helps ensure that on the day of judgment, we will remember our names.

The Bottom Line | THURSDAY

Shemoneh Esrei concludes with the verse: "May the words of my mouth and thoughts of my heart find favor before You, Hashem, my Stronghold and my Redeemer" (*Tehillim* 19:15).

This verse is generally considered to mark the end of *Shemoneh Esrei*. But this raises a question: When is the official end of *Shemoneh Esrei*? Is it when we complete the last *bracha* or after we have finished saying all of the concluding prayers before we take three steps backwards?

One opinion in the Talmud implies that this verse should be said as soon as we finish the nineteen blessings of *Shemoneh Esrei* (*Brachos* 9b). Based on this opinion, the *Shulchan Aruch* rules that it should be said immediately upon completing the last *bracha*. Before saying this verse, it is forbidden to say anything else (*Shulchan Aruch* 122: 1–2).

However, a second opinion in the Talmud implies that *yihyu l'ratzon* can be said after the prayers following *Shemoneh Esrei* (*Brachos* 29b). Based on this opinion, the Rema notes that in some communities the custom is not to say this verse until one is ready to take three steps backwards (*Rema* 122,1). Although many Ashkenazim follow the ruling of the Rema not to say *yihyu l'ratzon* until the very end of *tefilla*, the custom is to say the verse before responding to *kaddish* or *Kedusha*.

The Divine Presence | FRIDAY

"Whoever accustoms himself to saying four things will merit to receive the *Shechina*: 'Act for the sake of Your Name, Act for the sake of Your Right Hand, Act for the sake of Your *Kedusha*, Act for the sake of Your Torah'" (*Shulchan Aruch* 122,3). These four requests are inserted into the *Elokai Natzor* passage. What is so special about these four requests that they deserve such a rich reward?

Our Sages call this world darkness. Hashem has hidden Himself in the world so that only those who actively seek Him out will find Him. Yet He has given us a few tools to help us in this process: His Names, His Right Hand, His *Kedusha* and His Torah.

As physical beings, it is difficult to connect with Hashem, Who is completely spiritual. However, His Names are descriptions of His attributes, and they can help us to understand His actions in this world. Whenever we mention His Names, we come closer to Him, and our relationship is reinforced.

Some of Hashem's Names describe His kindness, while others describe His attribute of strict justice. Since we are not able to fathom the depth of His ways, too much harsh treatment could challenge our faith. Hashem's Right Hand represents His kindness, which is always extended to bring us back to Him.

We cannot help but like someone who makes the effort to understand us and fulfill our desires. Torah is the expression of Hashem's will in this world, and its study and fulfillment is the purpose of creation. When every action of our lives is in accordance with His will, we are drawn very close to Him.

The word "*kedusha,*" holiness, literally means separation. After perceiving a glimpse of Hashem's greatness through His Names, Right Hand and Torah, we recognize how different and distinct Hashem is from everything in creation. At that moment we experience a taste of *kedusha*, and we achieve the ultimate closeness to our Creator that is possible in this world.

At the conclusion of our prayers we mention these four tools, His Name, Right Hand, Torah and *Kedusha*. Our Sages promised that whoever does so on a regular basis will merit seeing the fruits of his labors. In the next world he will experience that which was impossible while confined to a physical body – he will merit receiving the Divine Presence itself (*Shulchan Aruch* 122,3).

As we conclude Shemoneh Esrei,
we have one last chance
to express the innermost chambers
of our soul.

18

Falling before Hashem

Understanding Tachanun Prayers against Pestilence

Covered Eyes | SHABBOS

Towards the end of his reign, King David instructed his general, Yoav, to travel throughout the Land of Israel and count all the people in his kingdom. After respectfully blessing the king that his nation should increase, Yoav questioned David's request. After all, does not the Torah tell us that counting the people brings a plague upon them, for only that which is hidden can receive blessing?

However, David was adamant and so Yoav and his men set out to complete their mission, traveling all over the kingdom of Israel, from the north to the south and the land east of the Jordan River. They counted the Jewish people in all the many towns. More than nine months later, Yoav returned to Jerusalem and presented King David with his census.

Suddenly David understood that he had done wrong and immediately begged Hashem to forgive him. That night

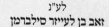

Hashem spoke to the prophet Gad and told him to go to King David and tell him to choose one of three punishments for his transgression. When he heard this prophecy, David said to Gad: "I am exceedingly distressed. Let us fall into Hashem's hand, for His mercies are abundant, but let me not fall into human hands" (*Shmuel* II 24:14).

By falling before Hashem in complete repentance, David chose the correct path. We see this because even though a plague of pestilence did indeed befall the Jewish people as a result of his decision, it was shortened to half a day instead of three.

In this incident, as in so many others, King David set a precedent with his service of Hashem that Jews continue to emulate to this very day. We likewise fall before Hashem during the daily *Tachanun* prayer, begging Him to draw us close to Him despite the fact that we have strayed. In addition, some have the custom to mention the above verse from *Shmuel* before starting to say *Tachanun*.

Some non-Jews pray with their hands together as if to show that without G-d their hands are powerless. During the *Tachanun* prayer we take this symbolism even further; we cover our eyes and put our heads down to show that without Divine guidance we cannot see or function (*Rabbeinu Bechaya, Bamidbar* 16,22). Let us try to understand the halachos and customs of this prayer where we literally fall into Hashem's hands.

Face-Down | SUNDAY

During *Shemoneh Esrei* we stand before the Divine Presence. Through each word and phrase, we elevate ourselves to one of the highest levels of connection that a Jew can achieve with his Creator while still in this world. What could possibly add to such an experience?

After praying seated and standing during *Pesukei D'zimra*, *Shema* and *Shemoneh Esrei*, our Sages described a final level of prayer as "*nefilas apayim*" - falling before Hashem. In its original form, *nefilas apayim* involved prostrating oneself on the floor as a sign of complete subjugation to Hashem's will.

The Zohar compares *nefilas apayim* to an act of *mesirus nefesh*, giving up our lives for Hashem's honor (*Bamidbar* 120b). For this reason some have the custom to say *vidui* beforehand, just as a person must do before he gives up his life *al kiddush Hashem*. In its original form *nefilas apayim* consisted of saying chapter 25 of *Tehillim*, which alludes to *mesirus nefesh*.

Since the Zohar warns that a superficial recital of *nefilas apayim* is potentially life-threatening, changes were made to how *Tachanun* is recited. Ashkenazim do not fall on the floor or recite chapter 25 of *Tehillim,* which mentions *mesirus nefesh*; rather, they put their heads down on their arms and recite chapter 6 of *Tehillim*. Sephardim recite the chapter of *mesirus nefesh*, but do not put down their heads.

In its initial form, *nefilas apayim* consisted of lying on the floor before Hashem. Since the Torah prohibits prostrating oneself face-down on a stone floor, it was necessary to tilt one's head and body to the side. Even after our way of saying *Tachanun* changed, the custom of turning one's head to the side remains (*Biur Halacha* 128,1).

The direction we should turn depends on how we are positioned in relation to the *Shechina*. The verse, "Hashem is your shadow on your right side" (*Tehillim* 121,5), implies that the Divine Presence is on one's right. Based on this verse, some opinions rule that a person should rest his head on his left arm, and turn his face to the right, so that he will be facing the *Shechina* (*Shulchan Aruch* 131,1).

On the other hand, the verse, "I place Hashem before me always" (*Tehillim* 16,8), implies that the Divine Presence is directly in front of a person. Some authorities maintain that when leaning on one's right arm and turning one's head to the left, a person faces the right of the *Shechina*, which is before him (*Tur* 131,1). When one's head is turned away from the left side of the *Shechina* and faces the right side instead, he fulfills the verse, "His left side is behind my head and His right side embraces me" (*Shir Hashirim* 2,6).

The Rema offers a compromise between these two options (128,1). In the morning, while wearing tefillin on one's left arm, in order not to rest one's head on the tefillin a person should lean on his right arm and face left. During *Mincha,* when one does not wear tefillin (according to most opinions), he should lean on his left arm and face right.

In Front of the Ark | TUESDAY

Tachanun marks a climax of prayer as we place ourselves in Hashem's hands. In order to reach such an elevated level we need some sort of external reminder that we are actually throwing ourselves down before Hashem. How can we achieve this?

"Yehoshua tore his clothes, and fell to the ground on his face before the Ark of Hashem ..." (*Yehoshua* 7,6). Throwing himself down before the Ark which contained the *Aseres Hadibros* helped Yehoshua internalize that he was "before Hashem." Based on Yehoshua's actions, we only say *Tachanun* face-down in the presence of a Torah scroll (*Rema* 131,2).

In Jerusalem a person can sense Hashem's closeness at all times. For this reason, some residents of Jerusalem have the custom to recite *Tachanun* face-down, even in a place where there is no *sefer Torah* (*Sefer Eretz Yisrael l'Harav Tukatchinsky* 1,9). Some explain that this only applies in the Old City, while in close proximity to the site of the *Beis Hamikdash* (Rav Shlomo Zalman Auerbach, as cited in *Ishei Yisrael* 25,39).

Dangerous at Night |

Our Sages describe the night as a time of justice and retribution. Under such circumstances the Zohar warns against falling before Hashem in *Tachanun* at night. Since the Divine attribute of judgment prevails, the results could prove spiritually dangerous.

At times a congregation's *Mincha* will extend until after sunset, a time when it is questionable if it is night or day. Some halachic authorities recommend that during this time one should recite *Tachanun* without leaning down on one's arm (*Mishna Berura* 131). This is the custom in Jerusalem and in other places outside of Israel (*Responsa Teshuvos and Hanhagos* 3,53).

At halachic midnight, the ascent towards dawn begins. During this time the strict judgment that prevailed earlier in the night starts to wane. Many authorities therefore permit falling down in *Tachanun* from midnight and onwards (*Mishna Berura* 131,18).

Women and *Tachanun* | THURSDAY

It is not customary for women to recite *Tachanun*. Some explain that the reason for this is similar to the reason that women do not recite *Maariv*. Since they were both originally optional prayers, women did not accept them upon themselves (*Tefillas Bas Yisrael* 2,12).

Others explain that *Tachanun* creates a situation where we pray in every possible position. *Pesukei D'zimra* and *Shema* are recited mostly while seated, *Shemoneh Esrei* while standing, and *Tachanun* in a bowed position. Since many halachic authorities rule that women are not obligated to say *Pesukei D'zimra* and *Shema*, they do not recite *Tachanun* either (*Machzeh Eliyahu* 20).

We may add that throwing oneself to the floor may be immodest for a woman. Since *Tachanun* originally involved falling before Hashem, women did not say this prayer. Even today, when the custom is to recite *Tachanun* while leaning on one's arm, women still do not say this prayer.

Uninterrupted Prayer | FRIDAY

One of the most famous disputes cited in the Talmud is between Rabbi Eliezer and Rabbi Yehoshua and relates to the halachic status of the oven of "*Achnai*" (*Bava Metzia* 49b). Rabbi Eliezer was so convinced of his position that he announced: "If I am correct, let a heavenly voice proclaim it so." Yet even after the heavenly voice verified that Rabbi Eliezer was correct, Rabbi Yehoshua maintained his position: "The Torah is not in Heaven! The Torah writes that the halacha is decided by ruling of the majority [who disagreed with Rabbi Eliezer], and therefore Rabbi Eliezer is incorrect!"

Although Rabbi Yehoshua was correct in his argument, since Rabbi Eliezer was saddened as a result, soon afterwards the world was afflicted with many different plagues. Rabban Gamliel, who was involved in the incident with Rabbi Eliezer, was caught in a storm at sea which threatened to sink his ship. Rabban Gamliel, who understood that this was a punishment for how he treated Rabbi Eliezer, asserted to Hashem that he had acted sincerely, and the sea calmed down.

Rabbi Eliezer's wife was Rabban Gamliel's sister, and she realized that prayer that comes from an anguished heart can be dangerous to the person who caused the pain. Since her brother had a part in causing her husband pain, she was afraid that Rabbi Eliezer's prayers posed a threat to Rabban Gamliel's life. From then on she interrupted her husband's prayers every day between *Shemoneh Esrei* and *Tachanun*, to prevent his prayers from being heard by Hashem.

One day Rabbi Eliezer's wife did not interrupt her husband's prayer, and her brother Rabban Gamliel died. While obviously this was a very unusual case, halachic authorities extrapolate from this incident that one should take the utmost care not to interrupt between *Shemoneh Esrei* and *Tachanun* since this can prevent one's prayers from being answered (*Shulchan Aruch, Taz, Gra* 131,1). Only other prayers are permitted during this time (*Mishna Berura* 131,1).

During Tachanun
we place our lives
into Hashem's hands,
and show that without His help
we cannot function.

19

Shemoneh Esrei Revisited

*Understanding
Chazaras Hashatz*

Pay Attention | SHABBOS

It was a regular Tuesday afternoon in the shul where the Rambam prayed *Mincha*, during the period when he lived in Egypt. The usual crowd had gathered for services, and a light-hearted atmosphere filled the air. As the *shaliach tzibbur* repeated *Shemoneh Esrei,* half the congregation was engaged in small talk, while the rest busied themselves with other matters.

For many years the Rambam had been filled with concern regarding the community's lack of respect for the repetition of the *Shemoneh Esrei*. That day his patience ran out, and the Rambam decided that what was going on was a *chillul Hashem*, a desecration of Hashem's honor. From that day onwards he decreed that *Shemoneh Esrei* would no longer be repeated in Egypt (as cited in *Responsa of the Radvaz* 1165).

Almost one thousand years later, we live in an age when technological advances have made information accessible to us

---

L'zecher nishmas
Miriam bas Menachem Mendel, Halevi

almost instantaneously, causing our attention spans to dwindle. If something is not packaged in a five-second sound bite, many people have difficulty finding the patience to hear it out. Listening to the entire repetition of the *Shemoneh Esrei* seems like an arduous task.

Yet the *Zohar* writes that the principal mitzva of *Shemoneh Esrei* is the *chazaras hashatz*, the prayer leader's repetition of this prayer. During *chazaras hashatz*, one member of the *minyan* represents the entire congregation to bring their prayers before Hashem.

Let us try to understand some of the customs and halachos of this crucial part of the prayer service.

Fulfilling One's Obligation | SUNDAY

When our Sages originally instituted the daily services, they knew that there were individuals who would not have the capacity to say the prayers. In order to ensure that everyone could fulfill the mitzva every day, they decided that during *Shacharis* and *Mincha*, *Shemoneh Esrei* should be repeated out loud. Individuals who did not know *Shemoneh Esrei* would listen carefully to every single word of the repetition and in that way fulfill their requirement of *tefilla*.

More often than not everyone in a shul knows the *Shemoneh Esrei*, and perhaps it can be argued there is no need for the repetition. Nowadays, literacy rates are very high and *siddurim* are readily available. Almost everyone can learn to say *Shemoneh Esrei*. It makes us wonder: Why did our Sages not stipulate that *chazaras hashatz* only needs to be said when there is someone in the shul who does not know how to recite it?

Our Sages understood that it was not practical to check before every service if there were people present who could not say *Shemoneh Esrei*. As in many other cases, they made a blanket decree that the *Shemoneh Esrei* must be repeated after every *tefilla*. By determining that the silent *Shemoneh Esrei* would always be followed by a repetition out loud, they ensured that whenever someone needed to hear it, he would have the opportunity (*Mishna Berura* 124,12).

In practical terms, if a person wants to fulfill his obligation to pray *Shemoneh Esrei* by listening to the *chazaras hashatz* he must understand Hebrew. He must stand with his legs together, as if he were reciting *Shemoneh Esrei* silently to himself, listen to every word recited by the prayer leader, and answer *amen* to every *bracha*. At the end of *Shemoneh Esrei* he should say *Elokai Natzor* and take three steps backwards (*Mishna Berura* 124: 3,6,23).

Listening |

Listening to *chazaras hashatz* is actually like reciting *Shemoneh Esrei* oneself (*Mishna Berura* 124,20). Therefore, if possible, a person should stand up while listening (*Rema* 124,4). Rav Shlomo Zalman Auerbach ruled that if one has difficulty standing, one can sit down for *chazaras hashatz*, but should try and stand for *Kedusha*, the start of *Modim*, and *Birkas Kohanim* (as cited in *Halichos Shlomo* 9,35).

If there are not nine people listening when the prayer leader recites his repetition, the blessings are considered almost to be in vain. No matter how many people are present in the shul, since many people have trouble concentrating at that time, each person should consider himself as one of the nine essential listeners. The prayer leader should have in mind that if there are not nine people listening, then his *tefilla* is a *nedava*, a voluntary offering (*Mishna Berura* 124: 17-19).

Half *Kedusha* |

As with other decrees of our Sages, there is more than one reason for repeating *Shemoneh Esrei*. Aside from aiding others to fulfill their obligation of saying *Shemoneh Esrei*, some maintain that the first and last three blessings of *chazaras hashatz* have to be repeated in order that *Kedusha* and *Birkas Kohanim* will be recited as a congregation. Since the beginning and end of *Shemoneh Esrei* must be said, our Sages decreed that the whole prayer be recited (*Aruch Hashulchan* 124,3).

There is an important halachic distinction between these two reasons. According to the first explanation, *Shemoneh Esrei* is repeated for the benefit of those who do not know how to recite it themselves, and so all nineteen *brachos* are equally important. Even if a person is pressed for time, there is no excuse to leave out any of them.

However, according to the second explanation, since *Birkas Kohanim* is generally not recited at *Mincha*, *chazaras hashatz* is primarily said so that *Kedusha* can be recited. If the hour is late or there is another pressing circumstance, it is sufficient for the congregation to hear the first three *brachos* of *Shemoneh Esrei* from the prayer leader, say *Kedusha*, and afterwards recite *Mincha*, without reciting *chazaras hashatz* afterwards. Some halachic authorities allow this practice during *Mincha* under particularly pressing circumstances (*Biur Halacha* 124,1).

Microphones |

Our Sages describe the enormous shul in Alexandria, Egypt. It was so big that the congregants seated at the back of the shul could not hear when the prayer leader finished reciting each *bracha*. Therefore, someone would hold up a large sign when the time came to answer *amen*.

Some modern-day shuls have a similar problem, though modern technology may offer a more efficient solution. During the week, at a time when there are many people in shul (e.g. Purim), perhaps the *shaliach tzibbur* can speak into a microphone. This way his voice will be heard throughout the shul.

Rav Moshe Feinstein concludes that while using a microphone during a weekday might be technically permissible, one should not use them in shul. Introducing microphones for *tefilla* could pave the way for other changes, which could present serious halachic problems (*Igros Moshe* 2,108). As far as reading the *megilla* is concerned, it is better to make two smaller *minyanim* than to hear the *megilla* through a sound system (*Igros Moshe* 4,126).

Noisy Shuls | THURSDAY

Non-Jews have reported that during their prayer services absolute silence reigns. A Jew, on the other hand, tends to feel at home in shul, and at times may feel comfortable enough to talk with his friends. Yet we should always remember that the mitzva to feel awe of the *Mikdash* applies in a shul, and we should be aware of Hashem's Presence at every moment.

The Torah instructs us to bring children to the mitzva of *hakhel*, the reading of the Torah by the king before the entire nation once every seven years, in order that they will be awed by the grandeur of this experience. Bringing children to shul can have the same effect, and can imbue within them a love and awe for the experience. While there, children should be taught to answer *amen* and to participate in the services as much as possible.

All this is on condition that the children are mature enough to appreciate the experience. Very young children run around in shul and disturb the rest of the congregation. Whoever brings them has taught them only that a shul is a playground and not a serious place of prayer (*Mishna Berura* 124: 27-28).

Too Much to Bear |

The *Shulchan Aruch* was written as a halachic guide and generally does not describe the severity of transgressions. Yet in regard to someone who talks during the *chazaras hashatz*, the *Shulchan Aruch* reveals that his sin is "too much to bear" (124,7). Why did the Shulchan Aruch make an exception for this halacha, and why is talking during *chazaras hashatz* referred to in such strong terms?

The source of this phrase is found at the beginning of *Bereishis*. After Kayin killed his brother Hevel, he was cursed by Hashem, banished from his home, and sentenced to wander the earth for the rest of his life. In response Kayin said that the punishment was "too much to bear" (*Bereishis* 4,13).

Halachic authorities write that the punishment for talking in shul is that the shul will be destroyed (*Mishna Berura* 124,27). A few hundred years ago there was an outbreak of massacres against the Jews of Europe. Rav Lipman, the author of the *Tosfos Yom Tov*, attributed these killings to the fact that Jews spoke in shul.

Man is created in Hashem's image and has a *neshama,* which is a part of Hashem Himself. As long as man is alive, Hashem dwells in this world. Killing another Jew is tantamount to banishing Hashem from this world.

Similarly, every shul is a miniature *Beis Hamikdash*, and is a dwelling place for the *Shechina*. As long as we maintain an attitude of respect and awe, the Divine Presence will dwell there. Talking in shul is tantamount to banishing Hashem from this world.

The *Zohar* writes that Hashem created this world in order that He should be able to dwell amongst man. Killing others and talking in shul share a similar outcome: we drive the Divine Presence from this world. Acting in a way contradictory to Hashem's desires in creating the world is "too much for Him to bear."

During the repetition of Shemoneh Esrei
we might feel the urge to talk.
Keeping in mind the severity of this
transgression can inspire us to try
to keep quiet and listen.

20

Leaping Souls

Understanding the Halachos and Customs of Kedusha

Heavenly Bound | SHABBOS

The Kotzker Rebbe once explained the quest for holiness in this world with the following parable: Hashem has fashioned a ladder that reaches from Heaven to earth, and souls descend on this ladder from the upper world to this one. The moment a soul reaches earth, however, the ladder is withdrawn; yet a heavenly voice summons the soul to climb back up to Heaven.

Some souls give up immediately. Since there is no ladder, they ask, how will they ever succeed in getting back up to Heaven? Other souls begin to jump towards Heaven, even without a ladder — but they too despair when they do not succeed after a number of leaps. Still other souls say to themselves, "Since there is no ladder, we are certainly obligated to leap and leap until at last G-d will have mercy on us and lift us up to Him" (*Leaping Souls* p. 138).

Perhaps no prayer better expresses our longing to return to our Heavenly home than *Kedusha*. We stand with our feet together

In memory of
Rosie Yaffah bas Rebbi Shimon Asil

as if we were angels and rise repeatedly to the tips of our toes in a leaping fashion, demonstrating our desire to get closer to Hashem.

Let us investigate some of the halachos and customs of this *tefilla*, in order that we may reach the threshold of the Heavens during our prayers.

Standing before Hashem | SUNDAY

"...I saw Hashem sitting on a throne ...*Seraphim* stood above Him; each one had six wings. With two he covered his face, with two he covered his feet, and with two he flew. And one cried to another and said, 'Holy, holy, holy (*Kadosh, kadosh, kadosh*) is Hashem, the earth is full of His glory.' And the posts of the door moved at the voice of him that cried..." (*Yeshaya* 6: 1-4).

If even inanimate doorposts trembled at the revelation of Hashem, certainly we should do the same. As a result, the custom developed to lift oneself up while saying *Kedusha*. While saying the phrases beginning with "*Kadosh*" (three times), "*Baruch*" and "*Yimloch*," one should lift his heels off the ground, in recognition of the awesome nature of standing directly before Hashem.

While the general practice is to lift oneself slightly off the ground, some people have the custom to jump up in the air. In doing so they are imitating the angels, who throw their entire essence into the task of glorifying Hashem (*Lavush* 125,2). However, a person should not jump during *Kedusha* unless that is the local custom, lest his behavior lead to ridicule (*Mishna Berura* 125: 7-8).

Connected Eyes | MONDAY

The eyes are the portal to the innermost chambers of the soul. Even if a person is in a crowded area, if his eyes meet with those of a close friend whom he has not seen in many years a feeling of closeness instantly envelops them. Suddenly, the distance has been bridged through the connection of souls.

While saying the words "*Kadosh, kadosh, kadosh*," Ashkenazim have the custom to lift their eyes towards the heavens. At that moment, there is as if the eyes of man and G-d meet, and it is a sense of great closeness between a Jew and his Creator. Hashem holds onto his Royal Throne, mentions the merits of the Jewish people, and hastens their redemption (*Mishna Berura* 125,5).

Looking Hashem straight in the eyes (as it were), is an experience of sublime *kedusha*, and some *poskim* advise that during this time one should keep his eyes closed (*Taz* 125,1). Others argue that one should keep his eyes open during this moment of intimacy. Most Ashkenazim follow the opinion that the eyes are open, while Sephardim keep them closed (*Mishna Berura* 125,6).

There are particular points in the services where we are invited to join the communal recitation of the prayers. *Barechu* - recited after the *kaddish* of *Pesukei D'zimra* - is one such point. The *shaliach tzibbur* summons everyone in shul to join him in the recitation of the blessings of *Shema*, the *Shema*, and *Shemoneh Esrei*.

The opening words of *Kedusha* function in the same way. The *shaliach tzibbur* introduces the *Kedusha* prayer and summons everyone to join him. For this reason, the *Shulchan Aruch* rules that the opening words should be said only by the *shaliach tzibbur* and not by the rest of the congregation (125,1).

The general custom, however, is to recite the entire *Kedusha*. Nevertheless, the phrases beginning with "*Kadosh*" and "*Baruch*" are the primary parts of *Kedusha*. Therefore, if a person is reciting *Elokai Natzor* at the conclusion of *Shemoneh Esrei* and he hears *Kedusha*, he should interrupt his recitation and respond only to these two phrases (*Mishna Berura* 125: 1-2).

If he is in the middle of *Shemoneh Esrei*, he may not answer *Kedusha*. Instead, he should listen to the recitation by the *shaliach tzibbur* of these two lines of *Kedusha*. Even though it is forbidden for him to join, he nevertheless fulfills the mitzva of *kiddush Hashem,* publicly sanctifying G-d's Name, by listening to these two lines of *Kedusha* (*Shulchan Aruch* 104,7).

A Chazzan's *Kedusha* | WEDNESDAY

While the *shaliach tzibbur* repeats the *Shemoneh Esrei*, there may be some people who are still in the middle of their silent recitation. These individuals may not speak, and they are obligated to listen to the *shaliach tzibbur's* recitation. The *shaliach tzibbur* should make sure to say the main lines of *Kedusha* out loud in order that those still in the middle of *Shemoneh Esrei* may fulfill their obligation.

What complicates matters is that some authorities rule that the *shaliach tzibbur* should say *Kedusha* together with everyone else, so that the *tefilla* is said by a *minyan*. If those still reciting *Shemoneh Esrei* are to hear *Kedusha*, the *shaliach tzibbur's* voice must rise above the voices of the congregants. If there are many people in the shul and the *shaliach tzibbur* does not think he can say *Kedusha* louder than them all, he should wait until the rest of the congregation has almost finished, and then say these lines of *Kedusha* (*Biur Halacha* 125,1).

Multiple *Kedushos* | THURSDAY

At times one may recite *Shacharis* early and spend the rest of the morning learning Torah in shul. If he is sitting in a shul that hosts one *minyan* after another, he may hear *Kedusha* every fifteen minutes! Must one interrupt one's learning to answer the *Kedusha* each time?

Every time one says *Kedusha* with a congregation he fulfills a mitzva of *kiddush Hashem*. While a person is not obligated to actively seek out this mitzva, if he encounters an opportunity he cannot forfeit it, even a hundred times a day. As long as a person is sitting in the shul and hears *Kedusha*, he must join in the response (*Igros Moshe* 3,89).

Sometimes a person walks by a shul where the congregation is saying *Kedusha*. Since he is not sitting together with that congregation, he is not obligated to stop and say *Kedusha* with them. However, it is still praiseworthy to answer (*Rema* 125,2).

Angelic Praise | FRIDAY

During *Kedusha*, we mimic the song that the angels sing to Hashem each day. Aside from the *Kedusha* that we say during the repetition of *Shemoneh Esrei*, we say *Kedusha* at the beginning of *Shacharis* — as part of the blessing of *yotzer ohr* before *Shema* — and again at the end of *Shacharis*, as part of *uva l'tzion*. For what reason do we say the angels' prayer, and why do we repeat it three times?

There are three points in *Shacharis* where we make major requests. The first is during the second *bracha* of *Shema*, when we ask Hashem for true success in Torah and mitzvos. Afterwards, in *Shemoneh Esrei*, we ask Him to take care of all of our physical and spiritual needs. At the end of *Shacharis*, during the prayer which starts *Uva L'Tzion*, we ask Hashem to let us see the final redemption.

Before we come in front of Hashem with requests, we are obligated to praise Him. Obviously, we can never sufficiently praise Hashem, and whatever praises we offer will inevitably fall short of doing justice to His glory. How can we ensure that our praises will be worthy?

While to some extent man is greater than angels, the angels have a much closer perception of Hashem's glory than mortal man. By repeating the praises they utter, we rise briefly to their perception and elevate our words. After offering such exalted praise, we can rest assured that our requests will find greater favor in Hashem's eyes.

*During the Kedusha prayer
our bodies and souls
tremble before Hashem.*

21

Blessing with Love
Understanding Birkas Kohanim

Hashem's Blessing | SHABBOS

My wife and I once found ourselves in an extremely difficult situation and went to discuss the problem with our *shadchan*, Rav David Cohen, Rosh Yeshivas Chevron, in Jerusalem. He told us that *Chazal* say that listening to ten *kohanim* say *Birkas Kohanim* is a powerful *segula*. Many people experiencing suffering and hardships have found relief after doing this.

Getting ten *kohanim* together at the same time was not an easy task, but my wife and I were finally able to do it. All of the *kohanim* showed up, and we received their *bracha* with hope and prayer that Hashem would help us. The very next day, we met the person who was instrumental in helping us solve our problem.

The source of Rav David Cohen's advice is in the *Zohar*: "During *Birkas Kohanim* the Divine attribute of mercy is strong throughout the world. Anyone who prays that their suffering should be removed will be answered" (*Naso* 147b).

In memory of
Chaya Dina bas Avrohom Yaakov (Iris Earl Frankel)

"And they [the *kohanim*] should put my Name upon the Jewish people and I will bless them" (*Bamidbar* 6,27). Perhaps there is no greater expression of Hashem's great love of *am Yisrael* than *Birkas Kohanim*. Let us investigate some of the halachos of this mitzva and understand how Hashem's devotion to His children is expressed through *Birkas Kohanim*.

Gazing through Windows | SUNDAY

"My beloved is like a gazelle or like a young hart; behold he stands behind our wall, he looks in the windows" (*Shir Hashirim* 2,9). This beautiful verse refers to Hashem's close relationship with the Jewish people. He constantly watches over us and has been with us at every point in our history.

The Hebrew word for "the windows" ("*hacharakim*") can also be read "five windows," because the first letter of the word, *hei*, not only means "the" but has the numerical value of five. This refers to the five windows that Hashem gazes through to view *am Yisrael*, His beloved children. Where are these five windows that Hashem peers through to watch over us?

While reciting *Birkas Kohanim,* the *kohanim* hold out their hands in a way that they create five openings with their fingers (*Shulchan Aruch* 128,12). *Chazal* reveal that the five windows hinted at in the above verse are these gaps. While the *kohanim* recite their blessing, the Divine Presence gazes fondly at us through these five openings (*Bamidbar Rabba* 11,2).

Bloody Hands |

"When you spread out your hands I will hide My eyes from you, even when you say your prayers I will not hear, for your hands are full of blood" (*Yeshaya* 1,15). It is considered inappropriate for hands that have been responsible for the death of another person to draw down Divine Blessings of love. Based on this verse, our Sages ruled that if a *kohen* has taken a human life he may not recite *Birkas Kohanim* (*Brachos* 32b, *Rambam Brachos* 15,3).

Someone was driving on an icy road when his car skidded and smashed into another automobile. The other driver was killed instantly by the impact of the collision. May the surviving driver continue to recite *Birkas Kohanim*?

The Rema rules that if he does *teshuva* he may continue to recite *Birkas Kohanim* (128,35). Therefore, if he is Ashkenazi and has undertaken a proper regimen of *teshuva*, he may continue to say this *bracha* (*Responsa Shevet HaLevi* 1,43). The *Shulchan Aruch* is more stringent, however, and Sephardim follow its ruling that the driver may not continue saying the *bracha* even though the death was an accident (*Shulchan Aruch* 128,35).

What is the halacha if the driver was driving recklessly? In such a case the death of the other driver is not considered accidental. While the *Shulchan Aruch* rules he can no longer recite *Birkas Kohanim*, according to the Rema, if he repents completely he may resume saying *Birkas Kohanim*.

A soldier returns from service in Iraq, where he killed a number of enemy soldiers. May he also return to his service blessing the Jewish people with *Birkas Kohanim*? Since he was fighting with the positive intention of protecting his country and the Jewish people, Rav Moshe Feinstein rules that he may certainly continue to say *Birkas Kohanim* (*Igros Moshe, Yoreh De'ah* 2,158).

Complete Concentration | TUESDAY

Birkas Kohanim is a close encounter with Hashem. Our Sages tell us that Hashem participates in the blessing, and that His Presence rests on the hands of the *kohen* (*Yerushalmi Sota* 7,2). The *kedusha* of the *kohen's* hands at the time of the blessing is so great that staring at them could weaken one's vision (*Rashi Chagiga* 16a).

Our Sages instituted special safeguards to ensure that the congregation would not be distracted during these auspicious moments. Someone who has visible physical deformities should not participate in *Birkas Kohanim*, for the congregants might be drawn to look at his hands. In addition to causing a person to lose his eyesight, the deformities could distract the congregation's attention from the blessing of the *kohanim* (*Mishna Berura* 128,109).

A painter, whose hands are generally decorated with dabs and smears of interesting colors, moves to a city where *kohanim* keep their hands outside their *talleisim* while reciting *Birkas Kohanim*. Since his colored hands could distract the members of the congregation, he should not recite *Birkas Kohanim*. However, if the local custom is to cover one's hands with a *tallis* during the *bracha*, or if everyone is already used to his multi-colored hands, the painter may recite *Birkas Kohanim* (*Shulchan Aruch* 128,32).

Dangerous Blessings | WEDNESDAY

In order for Hashem's blessing of love to be bestowed upon the Jewish people, there must be feelings of love between the *kohanim* and the congregation. The *Zohar* relates the story of a *kohen* who died because he did not recite *Birkas Kohanim* with good feelings (*Naso* 147a). In order to prevent such mishaps, right before reciting the blessings the *kohanim* make the *bracha*, "Who commanded the descendants of Aharon to bless His nation of Israel with love" (*Mishna Berura* 128,37).

Even though love is a prerequisite for *Birkas Kohanim*, the feelings of hatred must be quite intense in order to override the Torah mitzva of *Birkas Kohanim*. There was once a *kohen* who refused to accept the ruling of a *beis din*, and the community banned him from being called up first to the Torah. Nonetheless, the *Gedolim* of the time, while upholding this ban, ruled that he should still bless the congregation with *Birkas Kohanim* (Responsa *Mahari Asad, Orach Chaim* 49).

The *poskim* add that it is not sufficient that the relationship between the *kohen* and the congregation be hate-free. While making this blessing, the *kohen* is supposed to feel true love for the Jewish people, and they are supposed to feel love for him in return. Listening to the *bracha* of "Who commanded the descendants of Aharon to bless the Jewish people with love" should instill this feeling in our hearts (*Kaf HaChaim* 128,75).

Two Hands | THURSDAY

Many parents have the custom to bless their children on Shabbos evening with the verses of *Birkas Kohanim*. While doing so they place both hands on their children's heads. The *Zohar* explains that using two hands creates a complete connection between parent and child, allowing the full power of the blessing to flow into the child (as cited in *Responsa Yaavetz* 2,125).

Birkas Kohanim is a mitzva reserved exclusively for *kohanim*, and a non-*kohen* who recites it has committed a serious transgression. But doesn't the traditional Friday-night blessing violate this halacha? Are we not performing *Birkas Kohanim*?

Some authorities suggest that a non-*kohen* saying *Birkas*

Kohanim is only problematic if he does so with his hands spread out like a *kohen*. For this reason students of the Vilna Gaon would only rest one hand on their children's heads while blessing them (as cited in *Chumash Torah Temima Bamidbar* 6,23). This practice never caught on, and most parents continue to bless their children with both hands, though obviously not with the special openings between their fingers.

Of Prisons and Fires | FRIDAY

According to the Zohar, *Birkas Kohanim* is meant to be recited each time with the same joy that Aharon felt on the final day of the inauguration of the *Mishkan* (as cited in the *Aruch Hashulchan* 128,49). Some opinions say that an unmarried man may not participate in *Birkas Kohanim*, since without a wife he cannot experience true joy. Although halacha ultimately permits a single man to say *Birkas Kohanim*, he is permitted to abstain from reciting the blessing (*Rema* 128,34).

During the time of the *Rishonim*, a group of prominent Ashkenazic rabbis decreed that *Birkas Kohanim* should be recited only during *Yamim Tovim* (*Responsa Beis Ephraim* 6). The exact reasons for this decision are not known, but it is likely that it was connected to the intense hardships that their communities were experiencing at that time, which did not allow for them to feel joy. This ruling is upheld until this day and, outside of Israel, Ashkenazim recite *Birkas Kohanim* only on Yom Tov (*Rema* 128,44).

The Vilna Gaon and his students tried very hard to reinstate the daily *Birkas Kohanim*, but many obstacles blocked their efforts. In one instance the Vilna Gaon was arrested on false charges the day before a public *Birkas Kohanim* was planned. Rav Chaim of Volozhin, the Gaon's closest disciple, once tried as well. The night before the planned event, fire razed half the town of Volozhin, including the shul where *Birkas Kohanim* was planned (as cited in *Responsa Mashiv Davar* 2,104 and *Aruch Hashulchan* 128,64). Eventually these attempts were abandoned.

Jews will often travel great distances and spend a long time waiting in order to receive blessings from a *tzaddik*. While a *bracha* from a *Gadol* is very special, *Birkas Kohanim* offers us something greater and more powerful – a *bracha* directly from Hashem Himself. Whether we are able to hear it every day or only on the *Yamim Tovim*, *Birkas Kohanim* is a unique opportunity, and we should try to make the most of it.

> ## During Birkas Kohanim
> *Hashem gazes at us through the five windows created by the hands of the kohanim.*

22

Ending Well

Understanding Aleinu

Yehoshua and Achan | SHABBOS

Yehoshua led the Jewish people in their miraculous conquest of Eretz Yisrael. One of the most sublime moments of victory was when the walls of Jericho crumbled to the ground after the people encircled them for seven days. In expression of his awe and wonder at Hashem's greatness, Yehoshua composed the first paragraph of the *Aleinu* prayer at that time (*Kol Bo* 16).

At first, during Yehoshua's war against the nations who dwelled in the Land, there were no casualties among the Jewish people. However, later during the war against the city of Hai, the Jewish people suffered heavy losses. Afraid that this could cause a desecration of Hashem's Name, Yehoshua prayed for insight into the reason for this unexpected setback.

Hashem revealed to Yehoshua a number of reasons for these deaths, among them that one member of the Jewish people had violated the ban against taking spoils from battle at Jericho. When Yehoshua asked Hashem who the guilty party was, Hashem refused to divulge this information on the grounds that this was *lashon hara*. He advised Yehoshua to draw lots and find out for himself.

Yehoshua had the Jewish people draw lots, and eventually it became clear that Achan was the perpetrator of this offense. At first Achan denied his guilt, but when he saw that his defiance was causing violence among the Jewish people, he confessed. By transgressing Hashem's direct command that Jericho not be plundered, and by causing the deaths of his fellow Jews, Achan had committed a capital offense. He was sentenced to death.

Before willingly accepting his sentence, Achan confessed all of his transgressions and attained complete repentance. He expressed his newfound sense of closeness to Hashem by composing the second paragraph of the *Aleinu* prayer, an eloquent expression of Hashem's all-encompassing greatness. His authorship is hinted to in the first three words, "*al ken nekaveh,*" which share the same initials as his name, Achan.

The *Aleinu* prayer was thus composed by great *tzaddikim* at times when they were elevated by great love and awe of Hashem. Through a deeper understanding of the halachos and customs of this prayer, we too can access these feelings when reciting *Aleinu*.

Vanity and Emptiness | SUNDAY

"They bow down to vanity and emptiness and pray to a god who does not save them..." (from *Aleinu,* based on *Yeshaya*

45,20). The numerical values of the words *emptiness* (316) and *to a god who does not* (92) are identical to the names of specific individuals who espoused heretical beliefs. These hints were purposely inserted into this prayer in order to express disdain for their ideologies.

After non-Jewish authorities launched vicious attacks against Jewish communities due to *Aleinu's* insult to their supposed savior, censors worked relentlessly to have this line erased from the *siddur* altogether. Until this very day, there are some *siddurim* which print this part of the *Aleinu* prayer in parentheses or not at all. Since this verse is an integral part of *Aleinu*, one should make sure to include it.

For some people, even the slightest reference to heretical beliefs arouses such revulsion that they have a custom to pretend to spit before continuing with the next line, "and we bend down" (*Taz Yoreh De'ah* 179,5). This is meant as a symbolic gesture, and one should not actually spit in a way that could disgust others. Since one is acting for the sake of defending the Divine glory, this is not included in the prohibition against spitting in a shul (Steipler, as cited in *Orchos Rabbeinu* 1,68).

Bowing Down | MONDAY

"...and we bend down, bow, and give thanks before the King who reigns over kings" (ibid.). Pausing after the word *thanks* could imply a reference to the previous line, that we also bow down to vanity and emptiness. In order to emphasize the difference between our practice and that of others, one should pause between the words *who does not save them* and *and we bend down* (*Rema* 132,2).

Saying the words *and we bend down* in an upright position implies that one does not follow through with his words. In order to show that our actions are consistent with our stated beliefs, it is customary to bend over slightly while saying these words (*Mishna Berura* 132,9).

Need one bend his knees as well, as is the practice when reciting *Shemoneh Esrei*? The word "*korim*" ("bend down") implies bending one's knees, while the word "*umishtachavim*" ("and bow") implies bowing one's body. Once again, in order to ensure that their actions are totally consistent with our words, some bend their knees slightly while bowing (*Derech Hachaim* 132,2).

The Arizal revealed the tremendous importance of *Aleinu*, considering it a vehicle to bring down the *kedusha* of *tefilla*. He expressed this with a "*histachavayah gedola*," a particularly deep bow (*Be'er Heitiv* 132,4). On Rosh Hashana and Yom Kippur, during the repetition of *Shemoneh Esrei*, we take this one step further and prostrate ourselves on the ground while reciting these words.

When a group of Jews get together for prayer, they are paying public respect to Hashem. Sitting with them while occupied with something else shows a lack of respect for what they are doing. For this reason, someone who finds himself in a place where *Shema* or *Aleinu* is being said should recite them along with the congregation, even if he is not part of that *minyan* (*Mishna Berura* 65,9).

If a person is learning Torah in shul and he hears these prayers, must he interrupt his study and say them with the congregation? Since *Shema* is said sitting down, he is not showing lack of respect if he continues to sit and learn at that time. However, since *Aleinu* is said standing, if he would not get up and say it this would be a conspicuous deviation from the congregation. Therefore, one should interrupt Torah study to recite it (Rav Shlomo Zalman Auerbach, as cited in *Halichos Shlomo* 6,27).

Halachic authorities note that in most places, the individual does not recite every *tefilla* in unison with the congregation. *Aleinu* and the first line of *Shema*, however, should be said together. Since these prayers express the fundamental tenets of the Jewish faith, neglecting to say them with the group is tantamount to a denial (*Aruch Hashulchan* 65,6).

If a person is in the middle of *Shema* or *Pesukei D'zimra* and the rest of the congregation is saying *Aleinu*, he should not say it with them (*Responsa Minchas Yitzchak* 9,8). However, he should bow with the rest of the congregation when they say "*anachnu korim*" (*Aruch Hashulchan* 85,6).

The Order of *Aleinu* | WEDNESDAY

Depending on one's *nusach*, *Aleinu* is recited at a different point in the service. According to Ashkenazim, there are other prayers which follow it, while according to Sephardim and *nusach Sephard*, it is the final morning prayer. The different opinions regarding the placement of *Aleinu* are based on the reasons given for this prayer.

According to the Arizal, *Aleinu* envelops the rest of our prayers with a spiritual light, which prevents any forces of impurity from affecting them. It marks the conclusion of *Shacharis* and should always be the last prayer said in the morning. According to this understanding, if a Sephardi finds himself in an Ashkenazi shul, some maintain that he should still say *Aleinu* at the very end of his prayers as is his regular custom (*Responsa Vayeshev Hayam* [Rav Yaakov Hillel, *shlita*], 1,5).

On a more straightforward level, *Aleinu* fortifies our hearts with faith in Hashem, equipping us to face the challenges of daily life in this world (*Bach*). Based on this understanding, it need not be said as the very last prayer, and hence many Ashkenazim say other *tefillos* after it. However, since there is no reason not to leave it for the very end, if an Ashkenazi finds himself in a Sephardi shul, he should recite it together with them at the conclusion of *Shacharis* (Rav Shlomo Zalman Auerbach, as cited in *Mevakshei Torah* 5755: 166,68).

Technically, women are not obligated to say *Aleinu*. However, because of all of the reasons cited above and the great importance of this *tefilla*, it is proper for them to follow up their *Shemoneh Esrei* by reciting *Aleinu* (*Responsa Machzeh Eliyahu* 20). Some authorities obligate women to say *Aleinu* (Rav Yosef Shalom Eliyashiv, *zt"l*, Responsa *Kovetz Teshuvos*).

Leaving Early | THURSDAY

"At the end of our *tefillos*, we say the *Aleinu* prayer, standing with complete concentration" (*Rema* 132,2). "One should say *Aleinu* with fear and awe, for all of the Heavenly Hosts listen and Hashem stands with them. They all respond to the person reciting *Aleinu* by saying, 'Happy is the nation whose hope is in Him. Happy is the nation who Hashem is their G-d'" (*Mishna Berura* 132,8).

The Arizal reveals that while all parts of *Shacharis* generate a tremendous amount of *kedusha*, their effect on us is not immediate. When *Ashrei*, *Lamnatze'ach*, *uva l'Tzion* and *Aleinu* are said after *Shemoneh Esrei*, that is the time of "*yeridas hashefa*," the moment when all of the *kedusha* created by our *tefillos* comes down to us. If we leave shul before reciting them, the *kedusha* descends but does not find us (*Siddur Arizal*).

Occasionally, time pressures may force us to leave shul early for an urgent appointment. But if we find ourselves leaving early every day, we must understand that we are losing out on the fruits of our prayers. Every effort should be made to stay in shul until the very end of the services.

A Message from Above | FRIDAY

At one point during the Purim story, Mordechai decided to try and find out if he would be victorious in his struggle. He asked three children to tell him verses that they had learned that day. Such verses are said to have an inkling of prophesy and would indicate in which direction things were heading.

The first child said: "Be not afraid of sudden fear, nor of the ruin of the wicked, when it comes" (*Mishlei* 3,25). The second child said: "[Our enemies] take counsel together and it shall come to naught, for G-d is with us" (*Yeshaya* 8,25). The last child said: "Even in My old age I will carry you; even in My later years I will carry you, I have made and I will bear you, and I will carry and deliver you" (*Yeshaya* 46,4).

Mordechai understood that all three of these verses indicated that the Jewish people would be victorious and that their enemies would fall. Confident that these were Divine signs of his success, he continued his prayers and efforts. Eventually these prophecies were fulfilled, and the Jewish people prevailed in their struggle against Haman (*Yalkut Shemoni Esther* 1057).

Some halachic authorities mention the custom to say these three verses every day (*Taz*, end of *Orach Chaim* 132). In many *siddurim* they have been inserted after *Aleinu*. What is their connection to *Aleinu*?

Some commentators explain that *Aleinu* was established as part of our daily prayers to reiterate our belief in the One and Only G-d, since in the merit of this faith our prayers will be answered. Since this is the reward of such faith, *Aleinu* and these verses are said at the end of every *tefilla* (*Seder Hayom* p. 70).

Aleinu and these three verses are a final reminder before we leave the haven of the shul and go back to face our struggles, that the same message Mordechai heard so many years ago still applies to us today. No matter how bad things look, with Hashem's help the Jewish people will ultimately prevail. As ever, Hashem is guiding the course of history with an Omniscient Hand, and He will ensure that our prayers are answered.

*Aleinu sums up the message
of our prayers and gives us hope
that they will be answered quickly.*

23

The Beauty of Song

Understanding the Shir Shel Yom

Making Time for Song | SHABBOS

The Chasam Sofer was a Torah giant of the nineteenth century. He was both the Rosh Yeshiva and rabbi of Pressburg, a city that was home to one of the most important yeshivas and communities of his day. His halachic opinions were sought from across the Jewish world, and his numerous published works are still widely studied to this day.

Despite his devotion to Torah study and his busy schedule of communal responsibilities, music had a special place in his heart. Throughout his lifetime, the Chasam Sofer composed many songs expressing his devotion to Hashem. He once remarked that after Torah learning, the next best way to achieve genuine spiritual heights is through song

His son, the Kesav Sofer, was once asked where his father found the time to compose these verses. The Kesav Sofer replied that during the days between Yom Kippur and Sukkos his father

In memory of
Mrs. Genia Horn
From the Horn and Levine families

had been so totally overwhelmed with powerful feelings of love toward his Creator that he had difficulty learning Torah. In an attempt to give expression to the feelings in his heart, he penned those songs (*Nachlei Binah,* p. 8).

Music and song are a way to tap into our hearts and express our deepest emotions in prayer. When the Temple stood, every day the *Levi'im* sang the *Shir shel Yom,* a chapter of *Tehillim* that was relevant to that day. Their beautiful song was one of the most moving parts of the Temple service.

Today the Temple lies in ruins, and we cannot hear the beauty of that song. Our Sages ruled that we should say the *Shir shel Yom* every day to remind us of this void, in order that we should merit seeing the Temple rebuilt in our days (*Seder Hayom* p. 52). Thus, we conclude our morning prayers with the *Shir shel Yom* every day (*Rema* 132,2).

Let us look into the origins and customs of this practice so we can conclude our prayers with the same emotion and devotion as the *Levi'im* injected into their song.

Temple Song | SUNDAY

The song of the *Levi'im* was part of the *Korban Tamid,* the daily sacrifice. For almost 2,000 years we have been unable to perform this service or to hear the song of the *Levi'im*. Yet we keep the memory of this service alive in our hearts through the *Shir shel Yom*.

As part of this sacrifice, a *kohen* would pour a wine libation onto the altar. While he was holding the wine, a different *kohen* would stand next to him holding a flag. Two *kohanim* would stand on the table where the fat of the sacrifice was placed, and blow trumpets to alert the *Levi'im* that the moment for their song was near. When the *kohen* bent down to pour the wine, the other *kohen* holding the flag would signal to the *Levi'im* to start their song (*Tamid* 7,3, *Rambam Hilchos Tamidim* 6: 6 – 7).

Sundays and Wednesdays | MONDAY

Each day of the week, the *Levi'im* sang a different song that corresponded to what took place during the six days of Creation (*Tamid* 7,4). Following in their footsteps, every day we say the song that corresponds to that particular day. On Shabbos we recite the *mishna* which mentions all of the songs for the entire week (*Magen Avraham* 132,4).

"Hashem fills the earth and its fullness, the inhabited land and those who dwell in it" (*Tehillim* 24). On the first day of

Creation, the earth was created and Hashem was established as the Owner of everything, and on Sunday we start the week off with this song (*Rosh Hashana* 31a). Keeping this in mind helps us start off the week with the recognition that everything belongs to Hashem.

On the fourth day of the week Hashem created the sun, moon and stars. Although these luminaries were created to give light to the world, some people are drawn to deify them. In the future, G-d will punish those who worship them (*ibid.*), and for that reason on the fourth day we sing, "G-d of vengeance, Hashem" (*Tehillim* 94).

A Song of Vengeance | TUESDAY

The Temple was destroyed on a Sunday. According to the regular schedule of the *Shir shel Yom,* the *Levi'im* should have been singing, "Hashem fills the earth and its fullness." However, on the day that Hashem's house was to be desecrated, He did not deem it appropriate that the *Levi'im* should sing these words.

On that Sunday, a miracle transpired. Instead of singing the correct song for that day, the *Levi'im* sang the song for Wednesday, "G-d of vengeance, Hashem." At the last moment before terrible destruction would befall the Jewish people, Hashem wanted to give a sign that He would avenge what had taken place (*Eirechin* 11b).

The song of Wednesday concludes: "He will cut them off, Hashem, our G-d, will cut them off." While this was an appropriate message for our enemies at the time of the Temple's destruction, it is a harsh closing for us on a normal weekday. Therefore, we add the first three verses of the next chapter, "*Lechu niranana* – Come, let us sing to Hashem." In addition to concluding on a more pleasant note, saying these verses, which open *Kabbalas Shabbos*, remind us that Shabbos will soon be here.

Morning or Afternoon | WEDNESDAY

Why do we say these songs in the morning and not in the afternoon or evening, as is the case with other parts of the prayers that are repeated? The Beis Yosef writes that the appointed time for the *Levi'im* to say these *shirim* was in the morning. Therefore, we only say them in the morning (*Tur* 133).

Other commentaries note that the *Levi'im* did, in fact, sing their *shir* in the early afternoon. If so, why don't we say the *shir* during the afternoon prayers?

We can understand this practice in light of the fact that the *Levi'im* would only sing their song at the start of the afternoon. Since our custom is to recite their *shir* at the end *Shacharis* at the conclusion of our prayers, saying the *shir* at the start of the afternoon prayers would create a divergence of practices.

Therefore, the custom is only to say the *shir* in the morning (*Magen Avraham* 133,4).

On the morning of Tisha B'Av, when we are totally consumed with mourning the Temple's destruction, we do not recite *shir*. Tisha B'Av afternoon is already a time of consolation, and we start off our prayers with the *shir* (*Kitzur Shulchan Aruch* 124,19). Following the practice of the *Levi'im*, on Tisha B'Av we recite the *shir* at the start of the afternoon prayers.

Double Song | THURSDAY

Every weekday has a special song for that particular day. On Rosh Chodesh, Chanukah and other holidays, we are faced with the question of which *shir* to say. Should we recite only the special song for the day, or do we say the weekday song as well?

"When Rosh Chodesh falls on Shabbos, the song of Rosh Chodesh overrides the song of Shabbos. The song of Rosh Chodesh is given priority in order to publicize the fact that this day is the start of the new month" (*Sukka* 44b, *Rambam, Tamidim* 6,10). Based on this, the Vilna Gaon rules that when Shabbos or Chanukah coincides with Rosh Chodesh, we should only say the song of Rosh Chodesh (*Ma'aseh Rav* 157).

Others suggest that on regular days the *Levi'im* sang the normal weekday songs in the morning and on special days they sang extra songs during the *Mussaf* offering. Based on this, some maintain that the correct practice is to say the weekday *shir* after *Shacharis* and the festival *shir* after *Mussaf* (*Prisha* 133). However, since it is unclear exactly which songs were sung on Yom Tov in the *Beis Hamikdash*, it is preferable not to preface them with the phrase, "This is the song that the *Levi'im* sang in the Temple" (*Moadim U'Zemanim* 7,126).

A Song without a Song | FRIDAY

"How can we sing the song of a stranger on foreign soil" (*Tehillim* 137,4). When the Temple stood we had the opportunity to hear the beautiful song of the *Levi'im*. Today the *Shir shel Yom* serves as a substitute, but apparently the real *shir* is no more.

The Baal Shem Tov taught that even though the Temple now lies in ruins, we still have three kinds of song. The first type is a song with lyrics. While such a song can carry enormous spiritual power, it is still the lowest form of song, for its message is limited to the lyrics.

The second level of song is a tune without any words. Lacking any scripted message, this song transcends the first level. When one only hears a tune, his heart and imagination are free to draw their own inspiration from it.

The highest level of song is a song without a song – the

wellsprings of longing and hope that emanate from deep within our hearts. This is the highest level of prayer to Hashem. It is referred to at the end of *Shemoneh Esrei* as "*hegyon libi*," the meditations of my heart. It is a song with no words, no tune, no limits.

We have sung the Shir shel Yom
for so many years in exile.
Let us pray that the Temple
will be rebuilt soon,
and we will hear
the sweet songs of the Levi'im
once again.

24

The Last Word
Halachos of Answering Amen

Life or Death | SHABBOS

Rav Mordechai Yaffe, known as the Levush after his famous ten-volume work, was one of the foremost rabbis and Jewish leaders in Central Europe some four hundred years ago. He was offered the position of rabbi in the important Jewish community of Pozna, which he accepted on a single condition. Before starting his post he wanted to travel to Italy and study the laws of *ibur chodesh*, i.e. the knowledge of the lunar cycles necessary for understanding the calendar of new months and leap years.

Rav Yaffe spent some time in Italy studying under the great sage Mahari Abuhav until he had just about mastered this area of Torah. Towards the end of his stay, he happened to be in the house of his teacher when a child made a blessing on a fruit. Everyone answered "*amen*," with the exception of the Levush, who unintentionally neglected to respond.

The Mahari Abuhav was furious and declared a *nidoi*, a personal excommunication, against Rav Yaffe. For thirty days

לע"נ געלדה בת אשר זעליג פייגנבוים

the Levush remained isolated from the rest of the community, while the ban remained in force. At the end of the period, he went to the Mahari Abuhav to ask him to remove the *nidoi*. He also wanted to know why his oversight had merited such a harsh punishment.

The Mahari Abuhav said that at the moment that he had not answered *amen* to the *bracha*, a heavenly death sentence was issued against Rav Yaffe. The thirty-day ban had weakened the decree, and it could be completely overturned if the Levush and his descendants would undertake to teach the importance of answering *amen* to all *brachos*.

When speaking about *amen* the Levush was instructed that he should relate the following incident, which highlights the life-or-death power of the *amen* response:

There was a king who despised the Jews and was always looking for an excuse to banish them from his dominion. There was only one thing that prevented him from doing so: There was one pious Jew in his kingdom whom he liked and respected. This man was always successful in persuading the king to refrain from carrying out his wishes.

On one occasion the king was especially angry at the Jews, but once again the pious Jew subdued his wrath. A priest was present in the court at that time, and he proceeded to give the king a lengthy blessing in Latin. When he finished everyone answered "amen," with the exception of the Jew, who was in the middle of reciting Mincha and did not understand what had been said.

The priest was furious and said that because the Jew had not answered amen, the blessing would not come to fruition. The king's love of the Jew suddenly turned to hate, and he sentenced him to death on the spot.

Some time after his brutal execution, the pious Jew visited a surviving acquaintance in a dream and explained what he had done to merit such a terrible end. Once a child had made a bracha on bread in his presence, but the old Jew had not answered "amen." As a result, a heavenly decree of death had been decreed upon him, but had been held off until the incident with the king.

As his teacher annulled the ban against him, Rav Mordechai Yaffe undertook to teach the importance of *amen* for the rest of his life. Once a month he would fully recount the above incident, and he would often speak about the critical importance of responding to a *bracha* with *amen* (as cited in *Kaf HaChaim* 124,30).

The above stories imply that answering *amen* to a *bracha* is compulsory, and that the consequences are serious if one does not do so. This seems contrary to how many Jews behave in practice. Must one, in fact, answer *amen* to every *bracha* that he hears?

"When I mention the Name of Hashem, I will ascribe greatness to *Elokeinu*," (*Devarim* 32,3). Based on this verse, our Sages taught that every time a person hears a blessing, he is obligated to "participate" by responding *amen* (*Yuma* 37).

The above halacha applies only when a person is not involved with a different mitzva that requires his full intention. For example, if a person is studying Torah or in the middle of reciting other prayers, he is not obligated to stop to respond *amen* (*Eshel Avraham [M'Butchach]* 215).

A Child's Blessing | MONDAY

From the two above incidents we see that answering *amen* is mandatory even to the blessing of a child. However, the halacha specifies that one should only answer *amen* to the blessings of a child who has reached the age of *chinuch* and understands what he is saying. This implies that a younger child's blessing is not considered a *bracha*, and *amen* should not be answered (*Mishna Berura* 124,47; 215,16).

However, it is the widely accepted custom to answer *amen* to even a very young child's blessing. How can we reconcile this practice with the above halacha? Rav Chaim Zonenfeld suggested that any child who is old enough to make a *bracha* is considered having arrived at the age of *chinuch* with regards to *brachos* (*Responsa Simlas Chaim* 134).

Rav Shlomo Zalman Aeurbach took a different approach to teaching very young children to answer *amen*. He would mumble a response that sounded like *amen*, but did not say the actual word. In this way he would teach children the importance of answering *amen*, while not actually saying the word unnecessarily (*Orchos Rabbeinu* 3,223, [22]).

A Non-Jew's Blessing | TUESDAY

In the latter incident the pious Jew was sentenced to death because he did not answer *amen* to the blessing of the priest. Is one in fact required to answer *amen* to a non-Jew's blessing? Perhaps we should be concerned that his intentions are contrary to our beliefs?

"One should answer *amen* to the *bracha* of a non-Jew if one hears the entire blessing" (*Rema* 215,2). If a non-Jew uses the wording of *brachos* composed by our Sages, we can assume that he had the proper intentions when reciting his blessing, and respond with *amen* to his words (*Responsa Betzel Chachma*

3,39). However, the authorities clarify that answering *amen* to a non-Jew's blessing is optional and not obligatory (*Mishna Berura* 215,12. See also *Kaf HaChaim* 215,14).

Snatchers, Cutters and Orphans | WEDNESDAY

"A person should not answer *amen* that is *chatuf* (snatched), *katuf* (cut) or *yesoma* (orphaned)" (*Shulchan Aruch* 124,8). What are these interesting adjectives referring to?

The word *"amen"* must be pronounced properly, with both syllables correctly enunciated. Any *amen* that is incompletely pronounced is known as an *amen katufa* (a cut *amen*).

Additionally, an *amen* should only be said after the *bracha* has been completed, and not earlier. Any *amen* that precedes the conclusion of the blessing is known as an *amen chatufa*, a snatched *amen*.

A person may only say *amen* if he knows what *bracha* he is answering. Additionally, an *amen* response must always immediately follow the conclusion of the blessing. An *amen* that doesn't meet these two criteria lacks a connection to the *bracha* it is answering, and is called *amen yesoma* (orphaned *amen*) (*Shulchan Aruch* and *Rema* 124,8).

Someone in Israel received a call from his friend in the US, and while they were speaking, the caller in the US made a *beracha* on food that he was eating. Does the physical distance between them cause any *amen* answered to be "orphaned"? Authorities rule that even if two people are on opposite sides of the ocean, one may still answer amen to his friend's *beracha* if he does so immediately (*Igros Moshe, Orach Chaim* 4,91).

Matters of Life and Death | THURSDAY

In certain situations it is forbidden to make *brachos*, and if anyone hears a forbidden *bracha* he may not respond *amen*. While it is clear that this halacha applies to someone eating non-kosher food, Rav Shlomo Zalman Auerbach describes two other interesting applications.

When a person's close relative passes away, the mourner has the status of *onen* if there is no one else to arrange the burial. An *onen* is not obligated in mitzvos, and is not allowed to recite *brachos*. *Brachos* recited during this time are in vain, and one may not answer *amen* to them.

The other case applies to someone involved in saving a life. One example is an ambulance driver who gets an emergency call to rush to the home of a man who had a heart attack, and while driving grabs a bottle of water and, out of habit, makes a *bracha* before drinking. Since he is involved with saving a life, it is questionable whether he was allowed to make the blessing on the water, and it may be forbidden for those who hear it to respond *amen* (*Minchas Shlomo* 1,91,5).

"Whoever says *amen* with all of his strength merits to have the gates of Gan Eden opened up for him" (*Shabbos* 119b). "The moment a child says *amen* he has earned a place in the World to Come" (*Rema* 124,7 based on *Sanhedrin* 110b). What deep significance gives *amen* such a powerful influence in the World to Come?

"Any blessing that does not contain *Shem u'Malchus* (G-d's Name and Kingship) is not a *bracha*" (*Brachos* 12a). A *bracha* must mention Hashem, the Divine Name which represents His Mercy, and *Elokeinu*, the Name which represents Divine Justice and Majesty. The combination of these two Names encapsulates the way G-d relates to us in this world.

Whenever considering the Divine attribute of strict justice, we are at risk of forgetting that everything G-d does is absolutely good. In fact, even that which appears unpleasant to us is completely good, although we might not understand it at the moment. How can we ensure that we will remain steadfast in this essential principle of faith even while mentioning G-d's attribute of strict justice?

The halacha provides us with the answer to this question. *Amen* is an acronym for *El Melech Ne'eman,* G-d is a Faithful King. When we answer *amen* to a blessing we affirm that no matter how bleak things look, we can always rely on Hashem that all is for the best.

While a Jew should strive to see the good in every situation in this world, a complete understanding of this principle can only be attained in the World to Come. Our Sages say, "In this world we respond to bad news with a negative reaction. In the World to Come, we will say the *bracha* 'all that Hashem does is good' even on seemingly bad tidings" (*Pesachim* 50a).

While still in this world we can come closest to this perception by answering *amen* to all *brachos*, and affirming that Hashem is the *El Melech Ne'eman* in all situations.

May every amen help us
to attain the clarity
of the next world
while we are still here
in this one.

Glossary

Akeidas Yitzchak: Binding of Isaac

Aseres hadibros: Ten Commandments

Avinu: our father

Ba'alei teshuva: returnees to Judaism

Beis din: Jewish court of law

Beis Hamikdash: Holy Temple

Beis medrash: a study hall of a yeshivah

Bracha (pl. **brachos**): blessing (s)

Bris milah: circumcision

Chazal: acronym for *Chachameinu zichronam livrachah*, "Our Sages of blessed memory"

Chol hamo'ed: intermediate days of Sukkos and Pesach

Emunah: faith

Eretz Yisrael: the Land of Israel

Erev: eve

Gadol: a great Torah scholar

Gehenom: hell

Halacha (pl. **halachos**): Jewish law

Kabbalas Shabbos: accepting the Shabbos; prayers recited upon arrival of Shabbos

Kaddish (pl. **kaddishim**): sanctification prayer recited at end of a section of the prayer service

Kedusha: holiness; prayer

Kohen (pl. **kohanim**): priest(s)

Kohen gadol: high priest

Levi'im: Levites

Maariv: evening prayer service

Malach (pl. **malachim**): heavenly angels

Mezuzos: rolled parchments placed on the doorposts of Jewish homes, contains prayer of *Shema Yisrael*

Mincha: afternoon prayer service

Minyan (pl. **minyanim**): prayer quorum for ten adult males

Mitzva (pl. **mitzvos**): Torah commandment(s)

Moshiach: the Messiah

Neshama: soul

Piyutim: poetic prayers

Poskim: Rabbinic authorities on Jewish law

Rebbe: teacher

Rosh Chodesh: the beginning of the new Jewish month

Rosh Yeshiva: dean of a yeshiva

Sanhedrin: the highest court of Jewish law, currently not functioning

Sefer Torah: Torah scroll

Segula: useful (often kabbalistic) endeavor or charm

Shacharis: morning prayer service

Shechina: Divine Presence

Shir (pl. **shirim**): song(s)

Shir shel yom: song of the day

Shofar: ram's horn blown on Rosh Hashana

Sofer: scribe

Siddur (pl. **siddurim**): prayer book(s)

Shacharis: morning prayer service

Shaliach tzibbur: leader of prayer services

Shatz: acronymn for *shaliach tzibbur*, leader of prayer services

Shidduchim: the act of dating to get married

Tallis (pl. **talleisim**): prayer shawl(s)

Talmidei chachamim: Torah scholars

Tefilla (pl. **tefillos**): prayer(s)

Tefillin: phylacteries

Tehillim: Psalms

Teshuva: repentance

Tisha B'Av: the ninth of Av

Tzaddik (pl. **tzaddikim**): righteous person

Tzedaka: charity

Tzitzis: strings attached to a four-cornered garment

Vidui: confession

Yetzer hara: evil inclination

Yom Tov (pl. **Yamim Tovim**): Jewish festival(s)

"צו לי עלין אחי...ועמת לי מאוז"

ספר זה מוקדש
לע"נ ידידי נפשי הארי שבחבורה האברך החשוב

רבי אורי אפרים פרלמן זצ"ל
בן יבלחט"א הרב יוסף יצחק פרלמן שליט"א

שנקט בדמי ימיו בתאונת דרכים
בשנת העשרים וחמש לחייו

יגע ושקד בתורה יומם ולילה
הדיר שינה מעיניו
ודיו רב לו בש"ס ופוסקים
עניו וצנוע, שייף עייל ושייף
בנפיק מבושם במדות טובות
אהוב על הבריות
ורוח חכמים נוחה הימנו

נלב"ע יג טבת תשנ"ו

ת.נ.צ.ב.ה.

Praying
With
Joy

Who is wise;
He who learns from
every person.
From all my teachers
I grew wise.
(Pirkei Avos)

In honor of our parents
Herbert and Janice Hymanson,
our greatest teachers
Michael, Jerry and Susan

לעילוי נשמת

In Memory of

Ben and Julia Fernbach

wonderful parents and grandparents

The Cole and Fernbach families

Praying With *Joy*

לעילוי נשמת

Sonya bat Simha	Yankel ben Simha
Motel ben Chaim	Elie ben Simha
Khaskel ben Zalman	Mosya ben Zalman
Leah bat Shulem	Moshe ben Mosya
Chana bat Chaim	Chana bat Shmuel
Yosef ben Chaim	Emma bat Shmuel
Klara bat Chaim	Yakov ben Zakhar
Mika ben Chaim	Viktor ben Yarmolai
Zoya bat Chaim	Isohar ben Zakhar
Leib ben Simha	Rudolf ben Naum

Nelya bat Naum

by Saitskiy Family

Praying With Joy

לעילוי נשמת

In memory of my father
Mr. Paul Rosenzweig *z"l*
my mother in law
Mrs. Ingeborg Lichtenthal *a"h*
my father in law
Mr. Felix Lichtenthal *z"l*
and my late husband
Mr. Marc Lichtenthal *z"l*

May the tefilos of whoever
appreciates "Praying With Joy"
be answered speedily.

Dedicated by
Sharon Lichtenthal שיחי׳

In honor of my beloved wife Lauren
Who infuses simcha into our family
and serves Hashem with joy

Dedicated by
Rabbi Dr. Daniel Roth

לעילוי נשמת

In Memory of
R' Michel ben Moshe Baruch Goldmacher
Rochel Pesel bas Mordechai Goldmacher
R' Dov Dovid Gavriel ben Yehoshua Baruch Rubel
R' Yehosua ben Avraham Rubel
Tzipora bas Asher Zelig Rubel

סדר ברכת המזון

נוסח אשכנז

המזמן: רַבּוֹתַי נְבָרֵךְ.
המסובין עונין: יְהִי שֵׁם יְיָ מְבֹרָךְ מֵעַתָּה וְעַד עוֹלָם.
המזמן: בִּרְשׁוּת מָרָנָן וְרַבָּנָן וְרַבּוֹתַי, נְבָרֵךְ [כשיש עשרה: אֱלֹהֵינוּ] שֶׁאָכַלְנוּ מִשֶּׁלּוֹ.
המסובין: בָּרוּךְ [כשיש עשרה: אֱלֹהֵינוּ] שֶׁאָכַלְנוּ מִשֶּׁלּוֹ וּבְטוּבוֹ חָיִינוּ.
זימון לנישואין: דְּוַי הָסֵר וְגַם חָרוֹן, וְאָז אִלֵּם בְּשִׁיר יָרוֹן, נְחֵנוּ בְּמַעְגְּלֵי צֶדֶק, שְׁעֵה בִּרְכַּת בְּנֵי יְשׁוּרוּן, בְּנֵי אַהֲרֹן:
בִּרְשׁוּת מָרָנָן וְרַבָּנָן וְרַבּוֹתַי, נְבָרֵךְ אֱלֹהֵינוּ שֶׁהַשִּׂמְחָה בִּמְעוֹנוֹ, וְשֶׁאָכַלְנוּ מִשֶּׁלּוֹ.
המסובין: בָּרוּךְ אֱלֹהֵינוּ שֶׁהַשִּׂמְחָה בִּמְעוֹנוֹ וְשֶׁאָכַלְנוּ מִשֶּׁלּוֹ וּבְטוּבוֹ חָיִינוּ.

בָּרוּךְ אַתָּה יְיָ אֱלֹהֵינוּ מֶלֶךְ הָעוֹלָם. הַזָּן אֶת הָעוֹלָם כֻּלּוֹ. בְּטוּבוֹ בְּחֵן בְּחֶסֶד וּבְרַחֲמִים. הוּא נוֹתֵן לֶחֶם לְכָל בָּשָׂר. כִּי לְעוֹלָם חַסְדּוֹ: וּבְטוּבוֹ הַגָּדוֹל תָּמִיד לֹא חָסַר לָנוּ וְאַל יֶחְסַר לָנוּ מָזוֹן לְעוֹלָם וָעֶד. בַּעֲבוּר שְׁמוֹ הַגָּדוֹל. כִּי הוּא אֵל זָן וּמְפַרְנֵס לַכֹּל וּמֵטִיב לַכֹּל וּמֵכִין מָזוֹן לְכָל בְּרִיּוֹתָיו אֲשֶׁר בָּרָא. כָּאָמוּר פּוֹתֵחַ אֶת-יָדֶךָ וּמַשְׂבִּיעַ לְכָל-חַי רָצוֹן: בָּרוּךְ אַתָּה יְיָ. הַזָּן אֶת הַכֹּל:

נוֹדֶה לְּךָ יְיָ אֱלֹהֵינוּ. עַל שֶׁהִנְחַלְתָּ לַאֲבוֹתֵינוּ אֶרֶץ חֶמְדָּה טוֹבָה וּרְחָבָה. וְעַל שֶׁהוֹצֵאתָנוּ יְיָ אֱלֹהֵינוּ מֵאֶרֶץ מִצְרַיִם. וּפְדִיתָנוּ מִבֵּית עֲבָדִים. וְעַל בְּרִיתְךָ שֶׁחָתַמְתָּ בִּבְשָׂרֵנוּ. וְעַל תּוֹרָתְךָ שֶׁלִּמַּדְתָּנוּ. וְעַל חֻקֶּיךָ שֶׁהוֹדַעְתָּנוּ. וְעַל חַיִּים חֵן וָחֶסֶד שֶׁחוֹנַנְתָּנוּ. וְעַל אֲכִילַת מָזוֹן שָׁאַתָּה זָן וּמְפַרְנֵס אוֹתָנוּ תָּמִיד. בְּכָל יוֹם וּבְכָל עֵת וּבְכָל שָׁעָה:

סדר ברכת המזון

נוסח אשכנז

המזמן: רַבּוֹתַי נְבָרֵךְ.

המסובין עונין: יְהִי שֵׁם יְיָ מְבֹרָךְ מֵעַתָּה וְעַד עוֹלָם.

המזמן: בִּרְשׁוּת מָרָנָן וְרַבָּנָן וְרַבּוֹתַי, נְבָרֵךְ [בעשרה: אֱלֹהֵינוּ] שֶׁאָכַלְנוּ מִשֶּׁלּוֹ.

המסובין: בָּרוּךְ [בעשרה: אֱלֹהֵינוּ] שֶׁאָכַלְנוּ מִשֶּׁלּוֹ וּבְטוּבוֹ חָיִינוּ.

זימון לנישואין: דְּוַי הָסֵר וְגַם חָרוֹן, וְאָז אִלֵּם בְּשִׁיר יָרוֹן, נְחֵנוּ בְּמַעְגְּלֵי צֶדֶק, שְׁעֵה בִרְכַּת בְּנֵי יְשׁוּרוּן, בְּנֵי אַהֲרֹן:

בִּרְשׁוּת מָרָנָן וְרַבָּנָן וְרַבּוֹתַי, נְבָרֵךְ אֱלֹהֵינוּ שֶׁהַשִּׂמְחָה בִמְעוֹנוֹ, וְשֶׁאָכַלְנוּ מִשֶּׁלּוֹ:

המסובין: בָּרוּךְ אֱלֹהֵינוּ שֶׁהַשִּׂמְחָה בִמְעוֹנוֹ וְשֶׁאָכַלְנוּ מִשֶּׁלּוֹ וּבְטוּבוֹ חָיִינוּ.

בָּרוּךְ אַתָּה יְיָ אֱלֹהֵינוּ מֶלֶךְ הָעוֹלָם. הַזָּן אֶת הָעוֹלָם כֻּלּוֹ. בְּטוּבוֹ בְּחֵן בְּחֶסֶד וּבְרַחֲמִים. הוּא נוֹתֵן לֶחֶם לְכָל בָּשָׂר. כִּי לְעוֹלָם חַסְדּוֹ: וּבְטוּבוֹ הַגָּדוֹל תָּמִיד לֹא חָסַר לָנוּ וְאַל יֶחְסַר לָנוּ מָזוֹן לְעוֹלָם וָעֶד. בַּעֲבוּר שְׁמוֹ הַגָּדוֹל. כִּי הוּא אֵל זָן וּמְפַרְנֵס לַכֹּל וּמֵטִיב לַכֹּל וּמֵכִין מָזוֹן לְכָל בְּרִיּוֹתָיו אֲשֶׁר בָּרָא. כָּאָמוּר פּוֹתֵחַ אֶת-יָדֶךָ וּמַשְׂבִּיעַ לְכָל-חַי רָצוֹן: בָּרוּךְ אַתָּה יְיָ. הַזָּן אֶת הַכֹּל:

נוֹדֶה לְךָ יְיָ אֱלֹהֵינוּ. עַל שֶׁהִנְחַלְתָּ לַאֲבוֹתֵינוּ אֶרֶץ חֶמְדָּה טוֹבָה וּרְחָבָה. וְעַל שֶׁהוֹצֵאתָנוּ יְיָ אֱלֹהֵינוּ מֵאֶרֶץ מִצְרַיִם. וּפְדִיתָנוּ מִבֵּית עֲבָדִים. וְעַל בְּרִיתְךָ שֶׁחָתַמְתָּ בִּבְשָׂרֵנוּ. וְעַל תּוֹרָתְךָ שֶׁלִּמַּדְתָּנוּ. וְעַל חֻקֶּיךָ שֶׁהוֹדַעְתָּנוּ. וְעַל חַיִּים חֵן וָחֶסֶד שֶׁחוֹנַנְתָּנוּ. וְעַל אֲכִילַת מָזוֹן שָׁאַתָּה זָן וּמְפַרְנֵס אוֹתָנוּ תָּמִיד. בְּכָל יוֹם וּבְכָל עֵת וּבְכָל שָׁעָה:

וְהַקָּדוֹשׁ שֶׁנִּקְרָא שִׁמְךָ עָלָיו: אֱלֹהֵינוּ. אָבִינוּ. רְעֵנוּ זוּנֵנוּ פַּרְנְסֵנוּ
וְכַלְכְּלֵנוּ וְהַרְוִיחֵנוּ. וְהַרְוַח לָנוּ יְיָ אֱלֹהֵינוּ מְהֵרָה מִכָּל צָרוֹתֵינוּ.
וְנָא אַל תַּצְרִיכֵנוּ יְיָ אֱלֹהֵינוּ לֹא לִידֵי מַתְּנַת בָּשָׂר וָדָם וְלֹא לִידֵי
הַלְוָאָתָם. כִּי אִם לְיָדְךָ הַמְּלֵאָה. הַפְּתוּחָה. הַקְּדוֹשָׁה וְהָרְחָבָה.
שֶׁלֹּא נֵבוֹשׁ וְלֹא נִכָּלֵם לְעוֹלָם וָעֶד:

רְצֵה וְהַחֲלִיצֵנוּ יְיָ אֱלֹהֵינוּ בְּמִצְוֹתֶיךָ וּבְמִצְוַת יוֹם הַשְּׁבִיעִי הַשַּׁבָּת הַגָּדוֹל
וְהַקָּדוֹשׁ הַזֶּה כִּי יוֹם זֶה גָּדוֹל וְקָדוֹשׁ הוּא לְפָנֶיךָ לִשְׁבָּת בּוֹ וְלָנוּחַ בּוֹ בְּאַהֲבָה
כְּמִצְוַת רְצוֹנֶךָ וּבִרְצוֹנְךָ הָנִיחַ לָנוּ יְיָ אֱלֹהֵינוּ שֶׁלֹּא תְהֵא צָרָה וְצוּקָה בְּיוֹם
מְנוּחָתֵנוּ וְהַרְאֵנוּ יְיָ אֱלֹהֵינוּ בְּנֶחָמַת צִיּוֹן עִירֶךָ וּבְבִנְיַן יְרוּשָׁלַיִם עִיר קָדְשֶׁךָ,
כִּי אַתָּה הוּא בַּעַל הַיְשׁוּעוֹת וּבַעַל הַנֶּחָמוֹת.

בראש חודש ויו״ט וחול המועד וראש השנה

אֱלֹהֵינוּ וֵאלֹהֵי אֲבוֹתֵינוּ, יַעֲלֶה וְיָבֹא וְיַגִּיעַ, וְיֵרָאֶה וְיֵרָצֶה וְיִשָּׁמַע, וְיִפָּקֵד וְיִזָּכֵר
זִכְרוֹנֵנוּ וּפִקְדוֹנֵנוּ, וְזִכְרוֹן אֲבוֹתֵינוּ, וְזִכְרוֹן מָשִׁיחַ בֶּן דָּוִד עַבְדֶּךָ, וְזִכְרוֹן יְרוּשָׁלַיִם
עִיר קָדְשֶׁךָ, וְזִכְרוֹן כָּל עַמְּךָ בֵּית יִשְׂרָאֵל לְפָנֶיךָ, לִפְלֵיטָה לְטוֹבָה, לְחֵן וּלְחֶסֶד
וּלְרַחֲמִים לְחַיִּים וּלְשָׁלוֹם בְּיוֹם

בראש חודש **רֹאשׁ הַחֹדֶשׁ הַזֶּה.** בפסח **חַג הַמַּצּוֹת הַזֶּה.** בשבועות **חַג הַשָּׁבוּעוֹת הַזֶּה.**
בסוכות **חַג הַסֻּכּוֹת הַזֶּה.** בשמיני עצרת **שְׁמִינִי עֲצֶרֶת הַחַג הַזֶּה.** בראש השנה **הַזִּכָּרוֹן הַזֶּה.**
ילדים האוכלים ביום כפור **הַכִּפּוּרִים הַזֶּה.**

זָכְרֵנוּ יְיָ אֱלֹהֵינוּ בּוֹ לְטוֹבָה. וּפָקְדֵנוּ בוֹ לִבְרָכָה. וְהוֹשִׁיעֵנוּ בוֹ לְחַיִּים (טוֹבִים).
וּבִדְבַר יְשׁוּעָה וְרַחֲמִים חוּס וְחָנֵּנוּ וְרַחֵם עָלֵינוּ וְהוֹשִׁיעֵנוּ, כִּי אֵלֶיךָ עֵינֵינוּ, כִּי אֵל
מֶלֶךְ חַנּוּן וְרַחוּם אָתָּה.

**וּבְנֵה יְרוּשָׁלַיִם עִיר הַקֹּדֶשׁ בִּמְהֵרָה בְיָמֵינוּ. בָּרוּךְ
אַתָּה יְיָ. בּוֹנֵה בְרַחֲמָיו יְרוּשָׁלָיִם. אָמֵן:**

עַל הַנִּסִּים וְעַל הַפֻּרְקָן, וְעַל הַגְּבוּרוֹת, וְעַל הַתְּשׁוּעוֹת (וְעַל הַנִּפְלָאוֹת וְעַל הַנֶּחָמוֹת) וְעַל הַמִּלְחָמוֹת, שֶׁעָשִׂיתָ לַאֲבוֹתֵינוּ בַּיָּמִים הָהֵם בַּזְּמַן הַזֶּה.

לחנוכה

בִּימֵי מַתִּתְיָהוּ בֶּן יוֹחָנָן כֹּהֵן גָּדוֹל, חַשְׁמוֹנַאי וּבָנָיו, כְּשֶׁעָמְדָה מַלְכוּת יָוָן הָרְשָׁעָה, עַל עַמְּךָ יִשְׂרָאֵל, לְהַשְׁכִּיחָם תּוֹרָתֶךָ, וּלְהַעֲבִירָם מֵחֻקֵּי רְצוֹנֶךָ, וְאַתָּה, בְּרַחֲמֶיךָ הָרַבִּים, עָמַדְתָּ לָהֶם בְּעֵת צָרָתָם, רַבְתָּ אֶת רִיבָם, דַּנְתָּ אֶת דִּינָם, נָקַמְתָּ אֶת נִקְמָתָם. מָסַרְתָּ גִּבּוֹרִים בְּיַד חַלָּשִׁים, וְרַבִּים בְּיַד מְעַטִּים, וּטְמֵאִים בְּיַד טְהוֹרִים, וּרְשָׁעִים בְּיַד צַדִּיקִים, וְזֵדִים בְּיַד עוֹסְקֵי תוֹרָתֶךָ, וּלְךָ עָשִׂיתָ שֵׁם גָּדוֹל וְקָדוֹשׁ בְּעוֹלָמֶךָ, וּלְעַמְּךָ יִשְׂרָאֵל עָשִׂיתָ תְּשׁוּעָה גְדוֹלָה וּפֻרְקָן כְּהַיּוֹם הַזֶּה, וְאַחַר כָּךְ בָּאוּ בָנֶיךָ לִדְבִיר בֵּיתֶךָ, וּפִנּוּ אֶת הֵיכָלֶךָ, וְטִהֲרוּ אֶת מִקְדָּשֶׁךָ, וְהִדְלִיקוּ נֵרוֹת בְּחַצְרוֹת קָדְשֶׁךָ, וְקָבְעוּ שְׁמוֹנַת יְמֵי חֲנֻכָּה אֵלּוּ, לְהוֹדוֹת וּלְהַלֵּל לְשִׁמְךָ הַגָּדוֹל:

לפורים

בִּימֵי מָרְדְּכַי וְאֶסְתֵּר בְּשׁוּשַׁן הַבִּירָה, כְּשֶׁעָמַד עֲלֵיהֶם הָמָן הָרָשָׁע, בִּקֵּשׁ לְהַשְׁמִיד לַהֲרֹג וּלְאַבֵּד אֶת כָּל הַיְּהוּדִים מִנַּעַר וְעַד זָקֵן, טַף וְנָשִׁים, בְּיוֹם אֶחָד, בִּשְׁלֹשָׁה עָשָׂר לְחֹדֶשׁ שְׁנֵים עָשָׂר הוּא חֹדֶשׁ אֲדָר, וּשְׁלָלָם לָבוֹז. וְאַתָּה בְּרַחֲמֶיךָ הָרַבִּים, הֵפַרְתָּ אֶת עֲצָתוֹ, וְקִלְקַלְתָּ אֶת מַחֲשַׁבְתּוֹ, וַהֲשֵׁבוֹתָ לּוֹ גְּמוּלוֹ בְּרֹאשׁוֹ, וְתָלוּ אוֹתוֹ וְאֶת בָּנָיו עַל הָעֵץ:

וְעַל הַכֹּל יְיָ אֱלֹהֵינוּ אֲנַחְנוּ מוֹדִים לָךְ וּמְבָרְכִים אוֹתָךְ. יִתְבָּרַךְ שִׁמְךָ בְּפִי כָּל חַי תָּמִיד לְעוֹלָם וָעֶד. כַּכָּתוּב: וְאָכַלְתָּ וְשָׂבָעְתָּ וּבֵרַכְתָּ אֶת יְיָ אֱלֹהֶיךָ עַל הָאָרֶץ הַטֹּבָה אֲשֶׁר נָתַן לָךְ: בָּרוּךְ אַתָּה יְיָ. עַל הָאָרֶץ וְעַל הַמָּזוֹן:

רַחֶם נָא יְיָ אֱלֹהֵינוּ עַל יִשְׂרָאֵל עַמֶּךָ. וְעַל יְרוּשָׁלַיִם עִירֶךָ. וְעַל צִיּוֹן מִשְׁכַּן כְּבוֹדֶךָ. וְעַל מַלְכוּת בֵּית דָּוִד מְשִׁיחֶךָ. וְעַל הַבַּיִת הַגָּדוֹל

בַּמָּרוֹם יְלַמְּדוּ [עֲלֵיהֶם וְ]עָלֵינוּ זְכוּת, שֶׁתְּהֵא לְמִשְׁמֶרֶת שָׁלוֹם, וְנִשָּׂא בְרָכָה מֵאֵת יְיָ, וּצְדָקָה מֵאֱלֹהֵי יִשְׁעֵנוּ, וְנִמְצָא חֵן וְשֵׂכֶל טוֹב בְּעֵינֵי אֱלֹהִים וְאָדָם.

בשבת: הָרַחֲמָן, הוּא יַנְחִילֵנוּ יוֹם שֶׁכֻּלּוֹ שַׁבָּת וּמְנוּחָה לְחַיֵּי הָעוֹלָמִים.

בראש חודש: הָרַחֲמָן, הוּא יְחַדֵּשׁ עָלֵינוּ אֶת הַחֹדֶשׁ הַזֶּה, לְטוֹבָה וְלִבְרָכָה.

ביום טוב: הָרַחֲמָן, הוּא יַנְחִילֵנוּ יוֹם שֶׁכֻּלּוֹ טוֹב.

בראש השנה: הָרַחֲמָן, הוּא יְחַדֵּשׁ עָלֵינוּ אֶת הַשָּׁנָה הַזֹּאת לְטוֹבָה וְלִבְרָכָה.

בסוכות: הָרַחֲמָן, הוּא יָקִים לָנוּ אֶת סֻכַּת דָּוִד הַנּוֹפֶלֶת.

הָרַחֲמָן, הוּא יְזַכֵּנוּ לִימוֹת הַמָּשִׁיחַ וּלְחַיֵּי הָעוֹלָם הַבָּא. בחול מַגְדִּיל (בשבת ויו״ט אומרים מִגְדּוֹל) יְשׁוּעוֹת מַלְכּוֹ, וְעֹשֶׂה חֶסֶד לִמְשִׁיחוֹ, לְדָוִד וּלְזַרְעוֹ עַד עוֹלָם. עֹשֶׂה שָׁלוֹם בִּמְרוֹמָיו, הוּא יַעֲשֶׂה שָׁלוֹם עָלֵינוּ, וְעַל כָּל יִשְׂרָאֵל וְאִמְרוּ אָמֵן. יְראוּ אֶת יְיָ קְדֹשָׁיו, כִּי אֵין מַחְסוֹר לִירֵאָיו: כְּפִירִים רָשׁוּ וְרָעֵבוּ וְדֹרְשֵׁי יְיָ לֹא יַחְסְרוּ כָל טוֹב: הוֹדוּ לַיְיָ כִּי טוֹב, כִּי לְעוֹלָם חַסְדּוֹ: פּוֹתֵחַ אֶת יָדֶךָ וּמַשְׂבִּיעַ לְכָל חַי רָצוֹן: בָּרוּךְ הַגֶּבֶר אֲשֶׁר יִבְטַח בַּיְיָ, וְהָיָה יְיָ מִבְטַחוֹ: נַעַר הָיִיתִי, גַּם זָקַנְתִּי וְלֹא רָאִיתִי צַדִּיק נֶעֱזָב, וְזַרְעוֹ מְבַקֶּשׁ לָחֶם: יְיָ עֹז לְעַמּוֹ יִתֵּן, יְיָ יְבָרֵךְ אֶת עַמּוֹ בַשָּׁלוֹם:

בָּרוּךְ אַתָּה יְיָ אֱלֹהֵינוּ מֶלֶךְ הָעוֹלָם. הָאֵל. אָבִינוּ. מַלְכֵּנוּ. אַדִּירֵנוּ. בּוֹרְאֵנוּ. גּוֹאֲלֵנוּ. יוֹצְרֵנוּ. קְדוֹשֵׁנוּ קְדוֹשׁ יַעֲקֹב. רוֹעֵנוּ רוֹעֵה יִשְׂרָאֵל. הַמֶּלֶךְ הַטּוֹב וְהַמֵּטִיב לַכֹּל. שֶׁבְּכָל יוֹם וָיוֹם הוּא הֵטִיב הוּא מֵטִיב הוּא יֵיטִיב לָנוּ. הוּא גְמָלָנוּ הוּא גוֹמְלֵנוּ הוּא יִגְמְלֵנוּ לָעַד לְחֵן וּלְחֶסֶד וּלְרַחֲמִים וּלְרֶוַח. הַצָּלָה וְהַצְלָחָה. בְּרָכָה וִישׁוּעָה. נֶחָמָה. פַּרְנָסָה וְכַלְכָּלָה. וְרַחֲמִים וְחַיִּים וְשָׁלוֹם וְכָל טוֹב. וּמִכָּל טוּב לְעוֹלָם אַל יְחַסְּרֵנוּ:

הָרַחֲמָן, הוּא יִמְלוֹךְ עָלֵינוּ לְעוֹלָם וָעֶד. הָרַחֲמָן, הוּא יִתְבָּרֵךְ בַּשָּׁמַיִם וּבָאָרֶץ. הָרַחֲמָן, הוּא יִשְׁתַּבַּח לְדוֹר דּוֹרִים, וְיִתְפָּאַר בָּנוּ לָעַד וּלְנֵצַח נְצָחִים, וְיִתְהַדַּר בָּנוּ לָעַד וּלְעוֹלְמֵי עוֹלָמִים. הָרַחֲמָן, הוּא יְפַרְנְסֵנוּ בְּכָבוֹד. הָרַחֲמָן, הוּא יִשְׁבּוֹר עֻלֵּנוּ מֵעַל צַוָּארֵנוּ וְהוּא יוֹלִיכֵנוּ קוֹמְמִיּוּת לְאַרְצֵנוּ. הָרַחֲמָן, הוּא יִשְׁלַח בְּרָכָה מְרֻבָּה בַּבַּיִת הַזֶּה וְעַל שֻׁלְחָן זֶה שֶׁאָכַלְנוּ עָלָיו. הָרַחֲמָן, הוּא יִשְׁלַח לָנוּ אֶת אֵלִיָּהוּ הַנָּבִיא זָכוּר לַטּוֹב, וִיבַשֶּׂר לָנוּ בְּשׂוֹרוֹת טוֹבוֹת יְשׁוּעוֹת וְנֶחָמוֹת. הָרַחֲמָן, הוּא יְבָרֵךְ אֶת (אָבִי מוֹרִי) בַּעַל הַבַּיִת הַזֶּה, וְאֶת (אִמִּי מוֹרָתִי) בַּעֲלַת הַבַּיִת הַזֶּה, אוֹתָם וְאֶת בֵּיתָם וְאֶת זַרְעָם וְאֶת כָּל אֲשֶׁר לָהֶם. (אם סמוך על שולחן

עצמו יאמר: הָרַחֲמָן, הוּא יְבָרֵךְ אוֹתִי [וְאֶת אָבִי מוֹרִי וְאֶת אִמִּי מוֹרָתִי וְאֶת אִשְׁתִּי וְאֶת זַרְעִי וְאֶת כָּל אֲשֶׁר לִי], אוֹתָנוּ וְאֶת כָּל אֲשֶׁר לָנוּ, כְּמוֹ שֶׁנִּתְבָּרְכוּ אֲבוֹתֵינוּ אַבְרָהָם יִצְחָק וְיַעֲקֹב, בַּכֹּל מִכֹּל כֹּל, כֵּן יְבָרֵךְ אוֹתָנוּ כֻּלָּנוּ יַחַד, בִּבְרָכָה שְׁלֵמָה, וְנֹאמַר אָמֵן.

סדר שבע ברכות

בָּרוּךְ אַתָּה יְיָ אֱלֹהֵינוּ מֶלֶךְ הָעוֹלָם, שֶׁהַכֹּל בָּרָא לִכְבוֹדוֹ.

בָּרוּךְ אַתָּה יְיָ אֱלֹהֵינוּ מֶלֶךְ הָעוֹלָם, יוֹצֵר הָאָדָם.

בָּרוּךְ אַתָּה יְיָ אֱלֹהֵינוּ מֶלֶךְ הָעוֹלָם, אֲשֶׁר יָצַר אֶת הָאָדָם בְּצַלְמוֹ, בְּצֶלֶם דְּמוּת תַּבְנִיתוֹ, וְהִתְקִין לוֹ מִמֶּנּוּ בִּנְיַן עֲדֵי עַד, בָּרוּךְ אַתָּה יְיָ יוֹצֵר הָאָדָם.

שׂוֹשׂ תָּשִׂישׂ וְתָגֵל הָעֲקָרָה, בְּקִבּוּץ בָּנֶיהָ לְתוֹכָהּ בְּשִׂמְחָה, בָּרוּךְ אַתָּה יְיָ מְשַׂמֵּחַ צִיּוֹן בְּבָנֶיהָ.

שַׂמֵּחַ תְּשַׂמַּח רֵעִים הָאֲהוּבִים, כְּשַׂמֵּחֲךָ יְצִירְךָ בְּגַן עֵדֶן מִקֶּדֶם, בָּרוּךְ אַתָּה יְיָ מְשַׂמֵּחַ חָתָן וְכַלָּה.

בָּרוּךְ אַתָּה יְיָ אֱלֹהֵינוּ מֶלֶךְ הָעוֹלָם, אֲשֶׁר בָּרָא שָׂשׂוֹן וְשִׂמְחָה, חָתָן וְכַלָּה, גִּילָה, רִנָּה, דִּיצָה וְחֶדְוָה, אַהֲבָה וְאַחֲוָה וְשָׁלוֹם וְרֵעוּת. מְהֵרָה יְיָ אֱלֹהֵינוּ יִשָּׁמַע בְּעָרֵי יְהוּדָה וּבְחוּצוֹת יְרוּשָׁלַיִם, קוֹל שָׂשׂוֹן וְקוֹל שִׂמְחָה, קוֹל חָתָן וְקוֹל כַּלָּה, קוֹל מִצְהֲלוֹת חֲתָנִים מֵחֻפָּתָם וּנְעָרִים מִמִּשְׁתֵּה נְגִינָתָם, בָּרוּךְ אַתָּה יְיָ מְשַׂמֵּחַ חָתָן עִם הַכַּלָּה.

בָּרוּךְ אַתָּה יְיָ אֱלֹהֵינוּ מֶלֶךְ הָעוֹלָם, בּוֹרֵא פְּרִי הַגָּפֶן.